Employment Strategies for Career Success

Robert W. Rasberry
Southern Methodist University

Australia · Canada · Mexico · Singapore · Spain · United Kingdom · United States

Employment Strategies for Career Success
Robert W. Rasberry

Managing Editor:
Jack W. Calhoun

Editor-in-Chief:
George Werthman

Acquisitions Editor:
Jennifer L. Codner

Developmental Editor:
Taney H. Wilkins

Marketing Manager:
Larry Qualls

Production Editor:
Heather Mann

Manufacturing Coordinator:
Diane Lohman

Production House:
Lachina Publishing Services, Inc.

Printer:
Webcom
Toronto, Ontario

Design Project Manager:
Bethany Casey

Cover and Internal Design:
Bethany Casey

COPYRIGHT © 2004
by South-Western, a division of Thomson Learning. Thomson Learning™ is a trademark used herein under license.

ISBN: 0-324-20005-6

Printed in Canada
1 2 3 4 5 06 05 04 03

For more information contact South-Western, 5191 Natorp Boulevard, Mason, Ohio 45040. Or you can visit our Internet site at:
http://www.swlearning.com

ALL RIGHTS RESERVED.
No part of this work covered by the copyright hereon may be reproduced or used in any form or by any means–graphic, electronic, or mechanical, including photocopying, recording, taping, Web distribution or information storage and retrieval systems—without the written permission of the publisher.

For permission to use material from this text or product, contact us by
Tel (800) 730-2214
Fax (800) 730-2215
http://www.thomsonrights.com

Library of Congress Control Number: 2003101643

Dedication

My League of Friends

"It was my destiny to join in a great experience. Having had the good fortune to belong to the League, I was permitted to participate in a unique journey...."

For over two decades I experienced a unique journey with a League of Friends. Only in looking back over the years do I realize how, in many ways, we mirrored the story of one of my favorite college readings, *A Journey to the East*, by Herman Hesse. The journey took place in the summers of those years, as we consulted with the U.S. Chamber of Commerce's Institute for Organizational Management.

"There were wonderful festive days each time we encountered other parties of the League's hosts on our way; sometimes we then formed a camp of hundreds, even thousands." Our participants were executives from trade and professional associations and chambers of commerce from across the nation. We facilitated programs designed to help those leaders better serve their members, communities, and broader society.

"One of the characteristics of the Journey to the East was that although the League aimed at quite definite, very lofty goals . . . every single participant could have his own private goals." In reality our objective was to help participants keep their jobs and get new ones. I learned a lot about jobs, employment, and careers through my friends and those that we served. Over the years we saw people succeed beyond their wildest imagination, and fail in ways they had secretly feared. We all realized that knowing yourself, and the type of work you were meant to do, was critical before accepting a job. We also found that having a ready resume and a Plan B was a must. *". . . I then discovered how a long time devoted to small details exalts us and increases our strength."*

"It was not unusual for us to be mocked at and disturbed by unbelievers, but it also happened often enough that priests blessed us and invited us to be their guests, that children enthusiastically joined us, learned our songs and saw us depart with tears in their eyes; that an old man would show us forgotten monuments or tell us a legend about his district; that youths would walk with us part of the way and desire to join the League."

During the day the participants owned us. At night we had each other. Our campfire was a variety of restaurants that we grew to enjoy and return to. Our conversation was about the participants, the organization, and most of all ourselves and our families.

For most of us the journey recently came to an end. But the memories will continue throughout our lifetimes. This book is dedicated to my League of Friends.

Jerry Johnson—When we added up our time on the road, it equaled two years' worth of days. You kept me sane and taught me a valuable lesson: "Tell people what they mean to you while you have the chance. One day the opportunity will be gone." Jerry, I couldn't have asked for a better friend.

Margaret Fitch-Hauser—For a while you were the third musketeer, and our translator—cool, calm, and collected . . . every bit the model of Miss Manners. You made the journey truly adventurous, always looking for new places to go and things to explore.

Shannon Skousgaard—You were Leo, our leader. You argued our case with persuasive finesse. I admired you most for how you daily lived out your faith in a mighty and powerful way.

Janet Mills—Our road started at KU in an encounter group. From a project of baking bread to fine-tuning a program curriculum, I learned more about people from you than from all the books.

Jan Flynn—Although you joined the group late, your life experiences were inspiring and gave me practical answers to the most difficult job-related problems. You have a wonderful gift of giving.

Kichi Iwamoto—You started the journey and made us laugh, and each night dining was an adventure, for every meal was the "best that you had ever eaten."

Kip Lilly—Your classes were loud, your handouts busy, and you wisely refused the Power Point slides. But the vastness of your intellect amazes me. You are my Renaissance friend.

Frank Bonnelo—The most academic of us all. From the beginning to the end you never changed. From the academy to the economy, you gave us sound advice.

Fr. Steve Woolley—While you were with us you became our expert advisor . . . giving us insight on organizational culture and change. When you left for a "higher calling," we continued to be uplifted and blessed by your wisdom, meditations, and prayers.

What a journey we shared together . . . my League of Chamber Friends. I love you and thank you for the memories.

Robert Rasberry

Italicized words from Herman Hesse, *Journey to the East* (1988). Noonday Press.

Contents

Preface vii

1 Planning Your Career Path 1
  Get Acquainted with Your College Career Service 1
  Strategically Plan Your Career Center Use 3
  Self-Assessments and Inventories 5
  Occupational Investigation 16
  Pulling Your Career Plan Together 16
  Notes 18

2 Preparing Your Resume 19
  Contents of a Resume 19
  Three Kinds of Standard Resumes 28
  Constructing Your Resume 35
  Notes 44

3 Electronic Resumes 45
  Online Job Searching 45
  Electronic Resumes 49
  Notes 60

4 Employment Correspondence 63
  Letter Format 63
  Additional Employment Letters 70
  Notes 73

5 The Job Interview 75
  Preparing for the Interview 75
  Types of Interviews 78
  Types of Questioning Approaches 86
  Potential-Employment Tests 90
  Practicing for the Interview 95
  Making the Interview Count 95
  Notes 100

Index 103

Preface

Most of the college courses that you take, and books that you read, are focused on helping you survive in both your coursework and in the world of work. The objective of this book is to offer you some important information on an additional form of survival: the job search.

As an advanced business student, you and your peers—at school or at work—have many qualities in common. Each of you is well educated and able to apply coursework to your career. If you are not presently employed in a career-path job, you probably also share a desire to find that special job where you will be rewarded with top pay and praise for your contribution to the team. Do not be fooled into thinking that this special job will be easy to acquire, however. For the majority of students, obtaining the first major job takes a lot of hard work. Likewise, for those who are currently employed and working on a graduate degree, a new job—one that will allow you to use your newly acquired skills—is sometimes difficult to acquire.

Traditionally the job-search process required conducting a personal assessment, researching an organization, preparing a personal resume, writing letters of application, interviewing with several prospective employers both on and off campus, and sometimes applying for jobs through employment agencies. Some people still follow this approach. Today the process has been enhanced enormously by taking your job search online. Electronic job searching that was once used by only a few is now considered a critical job-finding alternative. In fact, employers are more frequently bypassing the campus recruiting process and are going straight to potential employees through their own online job-posting and resume-attaching services.

The goal of this book is to prepare you for whatever trials your job search may present. Chapter 1 outlines a method for planning your career path. It takes you through a process of clarifying who you are (personality and value assessment) and what you want to do (skill assessment and interest inventories). It will describe why you should make active use of all the career services your college has available, and it offers a four-year strategic plan for making that possible.

Chapter 2 shows you how to market yourself through the preparation of standard paper resumes: chronological, functional, and skills emphasis. Chapter 3 presents the argument of also using electronic resumes, and shows how to construct a scannable, e-mail, and Web resume. Chapter 4 describes how your marketing image is also enhanced through the writing of various types of employment-related letters.

While resumes and employment letters are crucial, they are marketing tools, and their primary objective is to help you obtain an interview. In Chapter 5 you will learn why the interview is important for both the company and you. The interview is your best opportunity to sell yourself to your prospective employer. The chapter describes types of interviews, types of interview questioning approaches, and lots of hints on making the event successful for both you and the company.

While the writing of a book is mostly an individual task, it can never be accomplished without the cooperation and help of many others. My thanks go out first to John Penrose and Robert Myers, my coauthors on another South-Western text, *Business Communication for Managers: An Advanced Approach*. Their generosity allowed me to use a portion of that book in this text. My thanks and appreciation also go to my loving wife, Jenni, and sons, Paul Michael and John Robert. You were all very understanding of my mood changes and absence during the long hours of writing. Without the help of my colleagues at South-Western/Thomson Learning the task would be incomplete. Thank you, Jennifer Codner, Acquisitions Editor; Taney H. Wilkins, Developmental Editor; and Heather Mann, Production Editor. I appreciate your organized manner and professional attention to detail. You have been a joy to work with.

Robert Rasberry has long held an interest in career planning. As a professor of Management and Organizations in the Cox School of Business at Southern Methodist University, he teaches leadership, ethics, and management. He takes an active role in counseling students regarding their career choices. As a former director of Communication Services in the Cox School, he and his associates developed career materials and gave personal feedback on resume development. As a trainer and consultant, he has conducted a popular seminar, "Finishing Strong," that encourages executives to find a healthy connection between job and family conflicts, and to create balance between success and significance. To undergraduates still active in job and career preparation, his advice is: "Don't major on your minor talents. Discover your strengths, perfect them, and success will follow."

Other Books by Robert W. Rasberry

Power Talk: Theater Techniques to Win Your Audience

Managerial Communication

Business Communication for Managers: An Advanced Approach

CHAPTER - 1

Planning Your Career Path

Anyone can find a job; finding the *right* job is harder. Finding the *right* job that will lead toward a successful and satisfying career is often very difficult. This chapter will focus on career planning, which is a process of finding a career that ideally fits your personality, intrinsic interests, values, job skills, and personal work style.

Career planning when approached correctly is a substantial part of life planning. Once you start planning the correct way, it will become an ever-evolving process and you will usually continue it all of your life. The end result will not be "dead-end" jobs, or a career path that frustrates and bores you. Instead, you will find work that daily presents exciting challenges and rewards. Getting there requires one thing: your willing and active participation. No one else can do personal career planning for you. It is your responsibility. Others can help and offer advice, but you have to evaluate and re-evaluate your dreams, interests, personality, skills, abilities, values, and goals. This chapter will get you off to a fast start if you are willing to actively participate.

If you are still in college you will have several career resources at your disposal. As a degree candidate, you also are faced with tremendous pressures. School administrators and placement center personnel push you early in your degree program to complete a resume, make a decision on your major area of emphasis, and start the interviewing process. All too often candidates do not consider what they want out of a job until, with resume completed, they find themselves in the middle of the interviewing season. With planning you will know what you want before developing your resume. If you do not, realize that you are competing with lots of fast-moving candidates who know exactly what they want in the job market. Take some time right now to assess your career potential and what you want to do. A trip to your college career office should be your first campus venture.

If you have graduated from college, or are not in school at present, the following information still will help you examine your strengths and desires in relation to jobs and a career. This chapter will also present lots of Internet sources that are available to you, even if a college career center is not.

Get Acquainted with Your College Career Service

A career advisor recently told me, "It's never too early—or too late—for a student to visit the College Career Office." Whether the office is called Career Development, Career Planning Services, or the Career Center, it is a one-stop shop for career advice. The staff is there to help you when you are deciding upon a major, researching companies, searching for an internship, writing resumes and cover letters, and preparing for interviews. Since your student fees have paid for their help, the service will also be FREE! Here is a list of career items a career center helps with, although the services at your specific school may vary.

- **Career Testing:** A series of self-assessment personality and skill inventories are usually offered along with professional interpretation.
- **Counseling:** Trained career advisors, who have heard almost every career problem or question, are there to talk with you. They will not find the right job for you or make contacts for you—but they will help guide you in using appropriate tools for your job and career search.
- **Alumni Interviews:** Previous grads that have become successful are great resources for jobs. They answer questions, give informational interviews, and often allow a student to "shadow" them at their work sites. The center usually has a long list of those who like to help students.
- **Alumni Services:** For prior graduates, who are in-between jobs, your alma mater career center still may provide you with job postings, resume assistance, and even career counseling. Some schools even have a reciprocal agreement with other colleges that allow you to use the career service of the school nearest you. Check with your alma mater and with the colleges in your area regarding such an agreement.
- **Career Library:** Career centers collect valuable books on the career search process, and gather information packets on companies that you can browse through. Staff members are also knowledgeable about how to navigate career Web sites and databases.
- **Help Guides:** Lots of career offices create their own career guides. Printed material ranges from information on how to get a job, how to complete resumes, interview techniques, multicultural resources, and other helpful items.
- **Internship and Co-op Programs:** These programs give you practical experience, expose you to real-life work situations, let you learn in real time, and apply classroom knowledge. Such an experience gives you a wonderful opportunity to observe a company in which you have a career interest, and it gives that company a chance to consider you as a permanent hire after graduation. Career centers keep an up-to-date list of the companies that have such programs available in their areas.
- **Employment Workshops:** Career centers offer a variety of scheduled workshops that investigate career opportunities, basics of job-searching skills, proper interview techniques, and ways of preparing for and taking graduate entrance examinations.
- **Recruiting:** Without a doubt this service is critical. Company recruiters go to campuses for on-campus interviews or career fairs. Career centers post schedules and host the on-campus information sessions and interviews.
- **Reference Service:** Some career services allow you to establish a confidential file of references from your past or present teachers, employers, and internship programs. These files are often retained and made available even after you graduate from the school.

Strategically Plan Your Career Center Use

Smart companies do not plan their goals and objectives quarterly, semiannually, or just once a year. Instead they develop long-term strategic approaches that cover several years. Each starts with a **vision** of what they want the company to be at a certain point in time. Next, they develop a **mission** that describes how that vision will be achieved in a precise, concise, and inspiring way. **Goals** that must be achieved to be successful are then developed. **Objectives** are established that are attainable, measurable, and that help them achieve their goals. All of these steps become a **strategy** for how resources and actions are used to insure effectiveness and efficiency in achieving the dream. Such a planning tool enables companies to stay focused on their desired vision, to become outcome oriented in prioritizing their actions, to integrate their work and resources around tasks and relationships, and to constantly be able to measure the distance between the present and the accomplishment of the future vision.

If you are a wise college student, the career center will not be a place that you go to your senior year just prior to graduation. Instead, it will be one of your first stops during the first semester of your freshman year. Develop your **vision** of having the ideal job at graduation. Construct a **mission** with four parts, where each year certain elements join together in helping you accomplish that vision. Set **goals** and **objectives**, where each class, and every workshop, will help you get closer to the final accomplishment of graduating with the ideal job and the promise of a wonderful career.

While you may be uncertain at this point about what you want to major in, and what you want to do for your life's work, the following road map will help dispel much of the fear and uncertainty.

Freshman Year

Use this year for self-assessments, to explore major options, and to become familiar with career planning activities. With the help of the career center staff take various psychological tests and career exercises. Collect, analyze, and evaluate all the information you can about your personality, abilities, skills, values, interests, academic training, and life experiences. From that information start constructing a career interest profile.

As you start considering a major area of concentration, start looking at courses that interest you. Talk with lots of people who are majoring in different areas. Ask questions about what they like about their majors, and what work they will be able to do with those majors. When you find people who have jobs and have already started their careers, talk to them about what they like and don't like. A great place to start this networking process is the campus career or job fair. You will learn lots about different industries, companies, and job opportunities. Start reading career and business publications. Investigate and join student organizations, especially the ones that focus on careers. Start creating a personal career action journal. Make notes on what you are learning. Give yourself assignments for things to search for in the career center. Keep articles and notes about short- and long-term career goals, and any other information about your career progress.

During the summer of your freshman year get a job that will give you work experience and will teach you how to get along with others. Ask lots of questions and try to learn all you can about career fields that interest you. By the beginning of your sophomore year strive to have answers to the following questions:

- What do I want to do for a job and as a career?
- What am I really able to do?
- Which career, at this point, would make me happy?
- What must I do to develop my competencies further?
- How will I be able to get the job I want when I graduate?

Sophomore Year

As you start this year narrow your career choice to two or three options. Your goal should be to make a decision on your career sometime during your sophomore year. Join new campus organizations that will give you added insight into your career development. Volunteer to help in those organizations and take on leadership responsibilities. Throughout the year read magazines like *Business Week, Fortune, Fast Company,* and *Business 2.0*. A subscription to one of those periodicals and to *The Wall Street Journal* will give you great information about work, different companies, corporate cultures, office politics, and career advancement.

Start honing your job-search skills by creating your resume, developing several cover-letter formats, and starting a contact and network list. Also during the year start researching internships, co-op programs, and study-abroad opportunities. Talk with a career counselor about which companies are right for your career goals. Continue to attend job fairs, and search out career workshops and job presentations.

In the summer try to fine-tune your work experience in a job within the primary career field that interests you. Continue to get good work experience and start building a reference list. As you start the beginning of your junior year, you should have answers to these questions:

- What skills and talents do I have to offer an employer?
- What companies need what I have to offer?
- What are two or three companies that I would love to work for?
- What must I do to make them want to hire me?

Junior Year

By this time you should be taking courses that fit your career path. From those courses you will gain valuable experience about companies and work. Continue your habit of regularly reading business periodicals. Spend time talking with faculty and career counselors to insure that you are on the right track. Continue developing your leadership skills through campus organizations and part-time work. Make it a habit to attend job fairs and career seminars. Obtain information interviews with alumni or leaders in your career area. Use friends and college personnel to help you network. Attend workshops on resume writing and cover letters. Polish your resume and start participating in mock interviews. Take advantage of internship opportunities and fine-tune your job-search strategy for your senior year. During the summer get a job in your chosen field. On the job find a mentor that will help you develop the maturity and knowledge you will need in your chosen field.

Ask lots of questions; seek lots of answers and suggestions. Before school starts shop for the appropriate attire that you will need for your senior year interviews and other career functions.

Senior Year

Start the year with an updated and polished resume. Realize that you will need to revise it later for the different jobs and opportunities you will consider. At the start of school identify the companies that will be interviewing on campus and start scheduling interviews. At the same time complete a list of select companies that you want to interview with but will need to contact. Visit with faculty, administrators, and everyone else who can assist you in your job search. Ask select individuals out of those groupings to serve as personal references who will later write letters of recommendation. You should always have at least three contacts available.

As you sign up for interviews spend lots of time researching the companies and developing interview questions that you would like to ask. Practice developing answers to interview questions that you learn that interviewers regularly ask. You will find sample interview questions in Chapter 5. As you interview assess your performance success. Make changes where needed. When you are invited for follow-up interviews look at the organizations discerningly. Send appropriate follow-up letters immediately after your interviews. When a job is offered, choose only the one that best fits your career vision.

If you will commit as a freshman to follow the above career planning process, you can be assured of having lots of job offers and of getting the ideal job that you desire. If you start the process in the middle of your college years you can still be successful, although you may have to cram lots of activities into short time periods.[1]

Self-Assessments and Inventories

Understanding yourself is a critical part of career planning. Regardless of when you start your career development program there are several assessment inventories or tests that you could benefit from taking. These instruments will give you an objective view of your personality, skills, values, interests, and work habits. The inventories are designed to give appropriate information and feedback about your life. You can find these inventories at your campus career center or testing service, and by searching the Internet. The tools used in the career center are always valid, while there can be concerns about whether the online material is reliable and accurate. One variable usually exists: The more-reliable tests usually carry a cost.

While most of the instruments are structured for easy interpretation, using the assistance of trained professionals allows you to apply your findings to majors, jobs, industries, and companies. If you have already spent time doing some personal assessment the results from the instruments may confirm your choices and alternatives.

Personality Inventories

Assessment in this area allows you to gain personal insight regarding your unique traits, attitudes, preferred work styles, interpersonal interaction patterns, and personal motivators/demotivators. Employers are increasingly using these tests to match applicants to jobs.

Myers Briggs Type Indicator (MBTI)
This is one of the oldest personality assessments available. Several forms of this instrument can be found on the Internet at **http://www.knowyourtype.com** although the version used by your career center should be valid. The original assessment is based upon the work of Carl Jung's theory of personality. The term "personality type" is used to indicate a person's predisposition toward behavior in four areas: Energized (extroverted or introverted), Attending (sensing or intuitive), Deciding (thinking or feeling), and Living (judging or perceiving). The instrument is used extensively in the organizational world to give employees insight into their personal behavior and the behavior of others. It is useful in describing behavior about how we learn, live, work, manage, and function with others. Reports generated from this tool help direct major, career, and employment decisions.

Keirsey Temperament Sorter
This inventory is based on the typology of the MBTI. David Keirsey developed the tool and made it popular in his book *Please Understand Me*. It has been widely used in employment training, premarital counseling, and relationship building. Lots of career centers use the test. You can take it free at **http://www.keirsey.com**. The 70-question assessment will give you results regarding your personality in the form of the MBTI descriptors. However, the language of temperaments—not type—is used. The four temperaments are: Guardians, Artisans, Idealists, and Rationals. Many people desire to take the MBTI first, and then review the Keirsey Web site for a comparative interpretation. The site is very entertaining and informative, and uses the work of Dr. Stephen Montgomery. In describing the temperaments he uses characters from popular books, movies, and TV.

Skill Assessment

Personal skills are natural abilities that have become talents, and learned abilities that you have acquired as a result of learning and knowledge. You might consider it a difficult task to identify your skills, although everyone has many of them. They are the activities you are good at. When you use a skills inventory assessment you identify two types of skills. **Transferable skills** are the ones that you have developed and acquired throughout your life. You have picked them up in places like classes, jobs, hobbies, or sports activities. They can be applied to a variety of situations. **Job-related skills** are technical skills you have developed. They are the skills you would use in specific jobs. Generally occupational skills are divided into three areas: Skills With Things, Skills With Information, and Skills With People. Most occupations require the blending of skills from all three areas.

Quality commercial skill assessments are limited. While a variety of free self-identity skill assessments can be found on the Internet, the most reliable commercial tool is part of the Strong Profile. **The Strong Interest and Comprehensive Skills Inventory (SCI)** describes how you *perceive* your own capabilities in performing tasks in six broad areas, called the General Occupational Themes. Since the tool reflects your perception and not your actual abilities, a true reading is not obtainable. The six areas are: Enterprising, Conventional, Social, Investigative,

Artistic, and Realistic. Interpretative materials available with the test describe typical majors, jobs, and job-related activities. Finally, your scores will identify four specific ways you prefer to approach courses or jobs: Work Style, Learning Environment, Leadership Style, and Risk Taking/Adventure.

As you begin your job search, it is important that you know your personal skills. Many career counselors approach the skill-assessment area by having participants self-identify their skills. You can do this by thinking back over your life and identifying several successful accomplishments at school, at work, and in volunteer organizations. You can then carry the exercise forward by considering what makes you happy and what you are good at doing.

For example, a typical term project in a class may have allowed you to develop and use several different skills. When you researched a topic you considered a way to search for specific information, conceptualize accomplishing objectives, and plan solutions for ways to present your research. If you did a project in an assigned team you had to make use of interpersonal skills, like cooperating, providing support, sharing credit, and being assertive. Perhaps you showed leadership skills through initiating new ideas, handling details, coordinating tasks, and managing conflict. When you wrote the final report you used communication skills of writing, reporting of information, persuading, editing, and orally making a presentation.

After you complete this memorable-accomplishments exercise, you will soon discover that you have a long list of skills that are transferable to future jobs. You can create your own checklist of skills by using the following items as a starting point. Table 1.1 gives you a sample framework in which to sort out the list.

- **Educational/Vocational programs** that you enrolled in, completed, and which contributed significantly to your overall education
- **Course work accomplishments** that were challenging and beneficial
- **Employment and jobs** that you were paid to perform and in which you learned specific skills
- **Volunteer, community, and extracurricular activities** that added to your skills, knowledge and leadership abilities
- **Personal hobbies** you have enjoyed
- **Military experiences** and jobs to which you were assigned
- **Recreational activities** you found exciting
- **Travel experiences** to different countries and the learning you acquired

After you finish the list, go back over the inventory and identify specific skills that you have especially enjoyed using in many of your different life activities and experiences. Create your own table to replace Table 1.1. As you review your new list—and probably longer inventory—circle the transferable skills that are apparent. Cluster the skills that you have listed repeatedly. In most instances the circled skills represent those that you will enjoy using in your career.[2] The National Association of Colleges and Employers (NACE) recently listed the essential skills identified by employers that it surveyed.[3] They are as follows:

- Communication skills
- Interpersonal skills
- Computer skills

Table 1.1 Functional Skills Transferable to Professional Employment

Communication and Persuasion	**Research and Investigation**
Writing concisely	Identifying problems
Listening attentively	Defining needs
Speaking effectively	Reading comprehension
Selling	Identifying resources
Interviewing	Data gathering
Facilitating discussion	Imaging alternatives
Negotiating	Solving problems
Persuading	Forecasting
Training	
Organization Management	**Human Relations**
Handling details	Interpersonal skills
Time management	Sensitivity to needs
Coordinating tasks	Listening empathetically
Decision making	Counseling
Coaching	Providing support
Counseling	Motivating
Delegating	Representing others
Meeting deadlines	Asserting
Coordination	
Administration	
Applying policies	**Information Management**
Giving directions	
Assuming responsibility	Math skills
Interpreting policies	Organizing information
Setting priorities	Record keeping
Promoting change	Attention to detail
Managing conflict	Logical ability
Selling ideas	
Design and Planning	**Work Survival**
Anticipating problems	Cooperating
Planning	Enforcing policies
Conceptualizing	Attention to detail
Seeking new ideas	Meeting goals
Visual thinking	Enlisting help
Anticipating consequences of action	Accepting responsibility
	Setting and meeting deadlines

Source: Adapted from *Stanford University Career Planning Guide*, (1995–1996, p. 14); and "Transferable Skills Sets," Quintessential Careers (3 pp.). Retrieved September 6, 2002, at **http://www.quintcareers.com/transferable_skills_set.html**.

- Motivational skills
- Analytical skills
- Teamwork skills
- Writing skills

Value Assessment

Your personal values are the things that are important to you, like achievement, order, status, and autonomy. Values become the inner standards from which we receive the motivation to act as we do, and by which we evaluate the behavior of others. In the work environment, "values" refer to how we feel about work itself and the contribution it makes to others in society. When we are able to do work that is congruent with our personal values, we feel successful and greatly satisfied.

Work values are divided into two categories: intrinsic and extrinsic. **Intrinsic values** refer to the actual process of working, the enjoyment that it produces, and the benefits that are generated both for us personally and for society. **Extrinsic values** relate to the favorable external work conditions that accompany an occupational choice, such as physical setting and earnings potential. To be truly satisfied in their work, most people need to find personal intrinsic value in that work.[4]

When we examine the lives of famous people we are often struck with how deeply their lives were guided by their personal values. For example, a famous lawyer was motivated by his commitment to social justice, and it led to his life work of appealing convictions of prisoners. A famous business CEO was motivated by the personal value that computers should be easy to use for the average person. Regardless of the personal values, it was ultimately their commitment and follow-through to implement the value in their lives that led to their great success.

Clarifying the things you value is another important step for you as you start the process of career planning. After you identify your most important values, you can search for organizations that stress those same values and that seek to hire employees with those same value sets. Table 1.2 will give you the opportunity to self-identify your values. Examine the list and put one check mark (✓) in front of the values that are important to you in your life, and especially in your work. Put *two* check marks (✓✓) in front of the values that are most important to you in your life and work. Be as honest with yourself as possible. You may find that you feel close to many or most of the listed values and that they are important to you. That's fine. But to develop a clear understanding of your life, of what makes you happy, and of the intrinsic values that you desire to use in work requires a deeper selection. After you have read through and marked the key values, select five most-important values and insert them in the designated space. Treat this exercise with seriousness and the results will help you in making proactive rather than reactive choices about career and job opportunities.

After you have narrowed your list of personal values, you will be able to use that list as you look at and sort out the differences in careers, organizations, and different jobs. The values that you cherish will have a direct impact on your job satisfaction, your career, and your life. Once you clarify what you value, you can better evaluate whether your current employer, or a prospective employer, supports your values. You will also be able to answer questions about future jobs like:

- Do I really want to supervise people?
- Do I want work where I cannot participate in team projects?
- Is a high salary the most important thing to me?
- Do I want a job where my work makes a contribution to society?
- Is working for a prestigious organization important to me?

Table 1.2 Clarifying What You Value

Ranking:
Evaluate each of the following values and put the appropriate check marks. Feel free to add any values of your own to the list.
1 check (✓)—Values that are IMPORTANT to me
2 checks (✓✓)—Values that are MOST IMPORTANT to me

_____ **Achievement:** Sense of accomplishment and mastery of projects.
_____ **Advancement:** Opportunities to move up and be promoted.
_____ **Adventure:** Duties that involve risk-taking, excitement, and unpredictable results.
_____ **Aesthetics:** Contributing to the beauty of things and ideas.
_____ **Affection:** Expression of love, concern, and caring.
_____ **Affiliation:** Participating with others in a group or network.
_____ **Appearance:** Concern for one's own attractiveness, or that of surroundings.
_____ **Authority:** Using power or control over the activities or destiny of others.
_____ **Broadminded:** Open-minded, tolerant, concerned with equality.
_____ **Change:** Work activities in which duties and projects change frequently.
_____ **Commitment:** Taking on pledges and obligations; being sold-out to the organization.
_____ **Community:** Living in a location that fits lifestyle and/or being involved in community affairs.
_____ **Competency:** Being capable and effective.
_____ **Competition:** Engaging in activities that pit your abilities against others; winning.
_____ **Cooperation:** Living and working in harmony with others.
_____ **Creativity:** Being innovative, imaginative; or creating new programs, materials, or structures; finding new ways to do something.
_____ **Decision Making:** Power to decide courses of action and policies.
_____ **Economic Return:** Working at a job that pays well.
_____ **Education:** An environment that promotes an appreciation for learning.
_____ **Fairness:** An environment that is just, where people are treated honestly and equitably.
_____ **Family:** Caring about parents, children, and relatives.
_____ **Fast Pace:** High degree of activity; work done rapidly.
_____ **Financial Gain:** Likelihood of achieving great monetary rewards for your work.
_____ **Flexible Work/Schedule:** Free to choose and work according to your own schedule.

(continued on next page)

Table 1.2 Clarifying What You Value (continued)

_____ **Freedom:** Free to choose thoughts and actions; independent and autonomous.
_____ **Friendship:** Close relationships with others.
_____ **Fun:** An environment that is playful in which you can receive pleasure and enjoyment.
_____ **Golden Rule:** Do unto others as you want done unto you.
_____ **Health:** Feeling of emotional/physical/spiritual well being.
_____ **Helping Others:** Doing work that benefits others.
_____ **Helping Society:** Contributing to improving the world.
_____ **Honesty:** Being truthful and sincere.
_____ **Independence:** Working on your own without lots of orders and direction being given from others.
_____ **Influence:** Having an opportunity or position to change attitudes or opinions of others.
_____ **Integrity:** Honesty, sincerity, and standing up for beliefs; walking your talk.
_____ **Intellectual Status:** Acknowledged as an expert possessing great abilities to learn, reason, and understand.
_____ **Intellectual Stimulation:** Work that requires lots of thought and reasoning.
_____ **Involvement:** Participating with others, belonging.
_____ **Knowledge:** Ability to engage in the pursuit of learning and understanding.
_____ **Leadership:** Directing, managing, facilitating, or supervising the work of others.
_____ **Leisure:** Having time to enjoy pleasure and relaxation.
_____ **Loyalty:** Displaying devotion to someone or something.
_____ **Management:** Planning, organizing, and supervising the work of others.
_____ **Material Status:** Gaining and possessing financial or material possessions.
_____ **Moral Fulfillment:** Work that contributes to a set of moral standards that are important.
_____ **Openness:** An environment that is receptive to new ideas and reason.
_____ **Order:** Being neat and organized; tranquility, stability, and conformity.
_____ **Peace:** Harmony; free from quarrels and disagreements.
_____ **Persuading:** Jobs that require personally convincing others to take certain actions.
_____ **Physical Challenge:** Jobs that require substantial physical activity.
_____ **Pleasure:** Seeking and receiving gratification; fun, laughter.
_____ **Power:** Having ability to influence or exercise control or authority.
_____ **Precision:** Jobs that require attention to detail and accuracy.
_____ **Prestige:** Having prominence, honor, and respect.
_____ **Problem Solving:** Jobs at which you can fix things and/or solve difficult tasks.
_____ **Public Attention:** Jobs in which you attract immediate notice because of appearance or activity.
_____ **Public Contact:** Day-to-day interaction with the public.
_____ **Quality:** Striving to improve all that you do.
_____ **Recognition:** Getting respect and approval for your work; having status.

(continued on next page)

Table 1.2 Clarifying What You Value (concluded)

_____ **Research:** Jobs in which you can search for and discover new facts and develop ways to apply them.

_____ **Respect:** Treating others with high regard and consideration.

_____ **Responsibility:** Being accountable for results.

_____ **Routine Work:** Work that requires little change and the following of established procedures.

_____ **Security:** Assurance of keeping your job and of receiving satisfactory compensation.

_____ **Self-Expression:** Use of natural talents or abilities that express who you are.

_____ **Self-Respect:** Pride and a sense of personal identity.

_____ **Supervision:** Jobs where you are directly responsible for the work of others.

_____ **Stability:** Work where duties are routine and largely predictable.

_____ **Teamwork:** Working together productively.

_____ **Time Flexibility:** Able to work according to your own schedule.

_____ **Travel:** Jobs where you frequently take trips.

_____ **Trust:** To have an assurance that those you rely upon and place confidence in will not fail you.

_____ **Wealth:** Making money, getting rich.

_____ **Wisdom:** Mature understanding of life, good sense and insight.

_____ **Working Alone:** Doing projects by yourself; limited contact with others.

_____ **Working with Others:** Being a team member and working toward a common goal.

_____ **Working with Your Hands:** Jobs where you can use your hands or hand tools.

_____ **Work Mastery:** Becoming an expert at what you do.

_____ **Work under Pressure:** Jobs where time pressure is prevalent.

_____ **Work with Machines or Equipment:** Jobs where you can use machines or equipment.

_____ **Work with Numbers:** Jobs where you use mathematics or statistics.

My Five Most-Essential Values

1. _____
2. _____
3. _____
4. _____
5. _____

Source: Adapted from: "Values," http://www.adm.uwaterloo.ca/infocecs/CRC/manual/values.html; "Clarifying What You Value," http://www.boeing.com/companyoffices/empinfo/wfreduction/Clarifying What You Value.html; "Checklist for Personal Values," http://www.uwec.edu/counsel/pubs/pvcheck.htm; and "The Power of Personal Values," http://www.gurusoftware.com/GuruNet/Personal/Topics/Values.htm.

You will find that just as individuals consider different values to be critical to their happiness and well-being, organizations also believe in a core set of values. Synovus Financial Corporation was the top selection in *Fortune* magazine's 1999 "100 Best Companies to Work for in America." Synovus's Web page on its corporate values states how the company views value differences: "We create an atmosphere where people feel respected, valued and appreciated because of, rather than in spite of, their differences."[5] Generally a company's values are listed in its company literature. Table 1.3 gives you a sampling of the core values of some of the larger U.S. organizations, and Table 1.4 presents six organizations with their described values.

Interest Inventories

Interest inventories show what you enjoy doing. When completed during career planning they give you a reading of your interests, aptitudes, and preferences. People in particular careers share similar interests. The results of an interest inventory will identify your preferences for particular activities. That information will then tell you how your choices fit with different careers and specific occupations. Three standard tools are most used for this purpose.

Campbell Interest and Skills Survey (CISS)

This instrument has long been used by counselors to survey a subject's self-interests and skills, to determine school subjects, varied work activities, and career occupations. One advantage of this tool is that it provides an estimate of the person's confidence in his or her ability to perform various occupational activities. It is excellent to use in gleaning major academic areas of study.

The **CISS** uses the following seven subsets and is able to direct the user to a variety of potential academic areas. For example:

Influencing	=	Leadership, Law, Political Science, Public Speaking, Sales, Marketing, Advertising
Organizing	=	Office Management, Supervision, Financial Services
Helping	=	Counseling, Medicine, Human Resources, Theology
Creating	=	Art/Design, Computer Graphics, Performing Arts, Writing
Analyzing	=	Math, Science
Producing	=	Engineering, Trades
Adventuring	=	Athletics/Physical Fitness, Law Enforcement, Military

Holland's Self-Directed Search (SDS)

This popular instrument, designed by Dr. John Holland, helps individuals find occupations that best suit their interests and skills. The Occupational Finder that accompanies the test contains over 1300 occupational possibilities. The Holland test is available in career centers, or you can self-administer it online at **http://www.self-directed-search.com/**. Dr. Holland contends that people work best in work environments that match their personality type. He has developed six interest areas: Realistic, Enterprising, Investigative, Conventional, Artistic, and Social. Most people are a combination of two or three of the Holland interest areas.

Table 1.3 A Sampling of Organizational Core Values

Commitment

Boeing	Saturn
Cadbury Schweppes	Starbucks
Herman Miller	Texas Instruments
Levi Strauss	Whirlpool
Nortel	

Fairness

Levi Strauss	Nortel
Marriott	TDIndustries

Fun

A.G. Edwards	Southwest Airlines
Hanna Andersson	Stride-Rite
Levi Strauss	USAA
Progressive	

Golden Rule

J.C. Penney	Servicemaster
Mary Kay	Synovus
Merrill Lynch	USAA
Progressive	

Honesty

Autodesk	TDIndustries
Guardsmark	USAA
Microsoft	

Integrity

Baxter	Levi Strauss
Boeing	Mary Kay
Ciba	Merrill Lynch
General Motors	Microsoft
Hewlett Packard	Procter & Gamble
Johnson Controls	Progressive
Johnson & Johnson	TRW

Leadership

Boeing	Levi Strauss
Cummins	Procter & Gamble
Ethyl	TDIndustries

Quality

Bayer	Thomas Cook
Hallmark	TRW
Hormel	Unocal
Intel	Whirlpool

Respect

Baxter	Saturn
Gallup	Starbucks
Guardsmark	Tom's of Maine
Nahser	Unocal
Rockwell	

Responsibility

Borg-Warner Security	Levi Strauss
Caterpillar	Nahser
Ciba	Nortel

Teamwork

Boeing	Mary Kay
Donnelly	Quad Graphics
General Motors	Saturn
GPU	USAA
Hewlett Packard	

Trust

A.G. Edwards	Quad Graphics
Hewlett Packard	Saturn
Hormel	Thomas Cook
Procter & Gamble	TRUSTe

Source: Adapted from Murphy, P. E. (1998). *Eighty Exemplary Ethics Statements.* South Bend, Indiana: University of Notre Dame Press.

Table 1.4 A Sample of Company Values

SOUTHWEST AIRLINES

- Profitability
- Low Cost
- Family
- Fun
- Love
- Hard Work
- Individuality
- Ownership
- Legendary Service
- Egalitarianism
- Common Sense/Good Judgment
- Simplicity
- Altruism

MICROSOFT

- Integrity and honesty
- Passion for customers, partners, and technology
- Open and respectful with others and dedicated to making them better
- Willingness to take on big challenges and see them through
- Self critical, questioning, and committed to personal excellence and self improvement
- Accountable for commitments, results, and quality to customers, shareholders, partners, and employees

BOEING

- Leadership
- Integrity
- Quality
- Customer Satisfaction
- People Working Together
- A Diverse and Involved Team
- Good Corporate Citizenship
- Enhancing Shareholder Value

INTEL

- Customer Orientation
- Discipline
- Quality
- Risk Taking
- Great Place to Work
- Results Orientation

THE GALLUP ORGANIZATION

- Respect for Talent
- Personal Development and Growth
- Pay for Performance
- Providing a Family-Friendly Environment

JOHNSON & JOHNSON

- Passion about the job
- Learning from and respecting one another
- Behaving with honesty and integrity
- Placing the customer first
- Being innovative thinkers and agents of change
- Thriving on mastering complexity
- Succeeding through interdependent partnering
- Supporting the development of people
- Valuing diversity of personal and academic backgrounds
- Maintaining work/life balance

Source: Adapted from Freiberg, Kevin, and Jackie Freiberg, "The Components of Southwest's Culture," *Nuts.* Bard Press: Austin, Texas, 1996, p. 147; "Microsoft's Mission & Values," **http://www.microsoft.com/mscorp/**, retrieved October 4, 2002; "Boeing: Values," **http://www.boeing.com/companyoffices/aboutus/mission/flash.html**, retrieved October 4, 2002; "Intel's Mission Statement, Values, and Objectives," **http://www.intel.com/intel/company/corp1.htm**, retrieved October 4, 2002; "Gallup's Workplace Values," **http://www.gallup.com/careers/work_values.asp**, retrieved October 4, 2002; "Johnson & Johnson: Sharing Core Values," **http://www.jnj.com/careers/difference.html**, retrieved October 4, 2002.

A fun version of the instrument's categories and career possibilities can be found online at "The Career Interests Game," http://www.career.missouri.edu/holland/. The game uses easy-to-remember terms for the six areas. In addition a person can observe personal characteristics, skills that they have, interests that they like, hobbies that display the interests, and career possibilities.

Strong Interest Inventory (SII)
This is another assessment tool that has been used for years. It measures interests in a broad range of occupations, work activities, leisure activities, and school subjects. The tool closely resembles both the **CISS** and the **SDS**, although the tools founder, E.K. Strong, Jr., was one of the pioneers in the development of interest inventories. The tool is excellent for individuals considering a career change, for employees seeking more satisfying work within an organization, and for students exploring career options. The inventory is a standard at career centers, or can be self-administered for a fee at **http://www.cpp-db.com/**.

Occupational Investigation

At this point in career planning lots of individuals need clarification regarding what they can do with a major in a particular discipline. This is where your campus career center shines. It will probably have printed materials available that will give you a complete understanding of all the various majors on campus. The center staff can discuss options with you and direct you to academic leaders on campus. Don't overlook your professors and other students in your academic departments and various classes.

You can survey career material online. Three different university career centers have posted excellent material on majors. Each gives an overview of the major, sample job titles and responsibilities, transferable skills that have been obtained elsewhere but apply to the majors, ways you can enhance your job potential outside the classroom, industry sources of information on the fields, basic resources for finding employment with the major, and a sampling of companies that have hired the individual majors from those schools. The Web sites for the university career centers are: **http://www.ashland.edu/cardev**, **http://www.udel.edu/CSC/op.html**, and **http://www.uncwil.edu/stuaff/career/Majors/**.

An excellent commercial Web site that is worth investigating is Quintessential Careers. It can be found at **http://www.quintcareers.com**. Search under the "Career Articles" section and you will find a great guide for researching companies, industries, and countries.

As you gather information about the new occupational options, start making notes that will help you with job resumes, employment letters, and job interviewing. You will need information on job descriptions, types of work environments, kinds of organizational training given to new hires, the overall future job outlook, employment trends in your targeted industries, compensation, and related occupations.

Pulling Your Career Plan Together

What do you want to do? Richard Bolles got into the career counseling business by accident over 30 years ago. Since that time his book, *What Color Is Your Parachute?*, has sold over seven million copies. It is updated yearly. Bolles divides his job-hunting process into three basic categories: (1) What do you want to do? (2) Where do you want to do it? (3) How do you get hired there? This chapter so far has offered suggestions on the first question.

It is now time to consider Bolles's second question, Where do you want to do it? Who do you want to work for? With the help of what you have learned about planning your career path, you are closer to being able to answer this question. The difficulty with answering it is that you must conduct extensive research on the organizations that interest you. If you do your research long before you write your resume and try to establish interview dates, you will come closer to knowing precisely which companies you do and do not want to work for. You will also prepare a resume and will be better able to ask and answer questions during your interviews.

As you proceed, the kind of work you want to do and whom you want to work for should begin to emerge. As you learn about different companies, consider how each one will fulfill you. For example, a 2000 study conducted by Watson Wyatt showed the seven highest-scoring items that workers under 30 most want from their jobs:

1. Compensation
2. Advancement opportunities
3. Flexible work schedules
4. Opportunities to learn new skills
5. Career development
6. Work at home
7. Use of competencies for career development.[6]

Do you identify with these motivators? Develop your own list, and then question whether the organizations that you are considering will allow you to meet your objectives.

If you answered, "Yes, the companies I have chosen to pursue for employment offer these motivators," then ask yourself five additional questions about each organization. These are considered classic job questions and were first posed by career specialist Edgar H. Schein:

1. Will this company give me the opportunity to stretch and really discover what I am capable of doing?
2. Will I really matter inside this organization? Will they see me as a person of worth? Will they give me real responsibility and a chance to show what I can really do?
3. Will I be able to maintain my integrity? Will this company help me achieve a balance in my life, to have a family, and to pursue my individual interests?
4. Will this job give me a real chance to grow? Will I be able to learn new things and develop new talents?
5. Will this company meet the ideals of the sound and ethical businesses that I have studied about? Will working for this organization enhance my self-image?[7]

If you have answered these questions affirmatively about a particular company and you are still interested in pursuing employment with that company, it is time to start your resume preparation and the interview planning. Chapter 2 begins that process.

Notes

1. Career planning and job search chart (n.d.). Retrieved March 22, 2002, at **http://www.black-collegian.com/career/archives/career.shtml**
2. Bolles, R.N. (2003). *What color is your parachute?* 30th ed. Berkeley, CA: Ten Speed Press. (If you are interested in a more-comprehensive examination of your skills, there are a variety of good career books which probably will be housed in your campus career office, or which you can find at a quality bookstore. Richard N. Bolles continues to be a wonderful source. His *The 2003 What Color Is Your Parachute?* devotes more than 100 pages to the topic. This book has been the premiere source for career planning for over 30 years.)
3. Developing a professional resume and cover letter that works. (n.d., 10 pp.). Retrieved March 22, 2002, at **http://www.black-collegian.com/career/resumecover2001-1st.shtml**
4. Values. (n.d.). Retrieved September 13, 2002, at **http://www.adm.uwaterloo.ca/infocecs/CRC/manual/values.html**
5. Corporate values. (n.d.). Synovus Corporation Web site. Retrieved September 14, 2002, at **http://www.synovus.com/index.cfm?subject=6&page=5**
6. Playing to win: strategic rewards in the war for talent—fifth annual survey report 2000/2001. Retrieved October 4, 2002, at **http://www.watsonwyatt.com/research/printable.asp?id=W-380**
7. Schein, E.H. (1964, November–December). How to break in the college graduate. *Harvard Business Review*, 68–76.

CHAPTER - 2

Preparing Your Resume

Is the resume important? Yes! It is the vital first step of your job-marketing program. As a job applicant, you may have excellent qualifications; however, if you cannot communicate your qualifications clearly in a resume, you may never reach the interview stage. Even if you are well-qualified, you may never have the chance to discuss those strengths with an interviewer if your resume is weak. A good resume is a marketing tool. It should portray you in the most favorable manner possible.

As a marketing tool, the resume's purpose is to SELL YOU! More precisely, the purpose is to interest the employer to the point of wanting to interview you. A resume will not get you a job. If prepared properly, it can get you an interview. Your resume should include the most important information about you at a certain time in your life. It is a written snapshot of who you are, what you want, and what you have achieved, demonstrated, and learned.

The word "resume" comes from the French verb meaning "to *summarize*"; your resume is a summary of pertinent facts about you. Writing a resume is an easy task—at first glance. Almost anyone can sit down for 30 minutes and produce a mediocre employment summary. Keep in mind that an employer spends about 30 seconds reading a resume before deciding whether to toss it or to consider it further. No wonder one corporate personnel officer said, "We get up to a hundred resumes a day; they all look pretty much the same. They lack what we really need to know; they are dull and boring. Guess where most of them end up?" Developing a strategic plan that focuses on what you want to do now and several years down the road will help ensure that your resume does not self-destruct with the others and that you get a fair shot at the job of your choice.

Contents of a Resume

Although most people agree on the general information that goes into a resume, there is some debate when it comes to the specifics. In fact, the Harvard University Graduate School of Business *Student Handbook on Resume Writing* states:

> Authorities differ as to exactly what should be included in a resume. A sound and proven fundamental approach is to consider your resume as a truthful sales presentation that you have prepared for potential employers. Since its purpose is to help you sell your services, it should include the facts about yourself that will give consistency and strength to your stated job and career objective.

Don't write an autobiography or an obituary; the resume is not an all-inclusive life history! In it you work mostly with the "plus factors" that will help you sell yourself, so emphasize your most important assets. Above all, it must be factual. Each statement needs to be accurate and not blown-up beyond its value; on the other hand, it need not be underplayed. Executives are seeking capabilities, so write up your achievements with the employer's needs in mind.[1]

Look back at the career planning you did in Chapter 1. By evaluating your career interests and exploring career options, you will be able to construct a resume that shows balance between the needs of a selected employer and your desires as a job candidate. Here is a good way to picture the balance of employer needs versus what you offer:

Employer Needs	Your Resume Description
Who are you?	*Identification* section
How can you be contacted?	*Identification* section
What do you want to do?	Job *objective*
What can you do?	Personal skills; *Experience* section
Who have you done it with?	*Employment* history
What have you learned?	*Education* section

To describe yourself on paper using the above concept requires being organized and precise. You will place this information in compartmentalized sections of your resume. The pages that follow list the standard resume areas that are considered mandatory for resume construction. Table 2.1 lists a sampling of headings that can also be used.

Table 2.1 Possible Resume Headings

Teaching Experience	Civic Activities
Coaching Experience	Community Service
Activities	College Activites
College Distinctions	Areas of Knowledge
Part-Time & Summer Work	Organizations
Capabilities	Career-Related Experiences
Course Highlights	Special Talents
Memberships	Leisure Activities
Professional Affiliations	Educational Interests
Travel Abroad	Travel
Language Competencies	Hobbies
Related Coursework	Scholarships
Special Training	Current Certification
Research Interests	Endorsements
Conferences Attended	Achievements
Accomplishments	

When you list information always be specific, avoid sketchiness, and state your most important and strongest facts first. Omit anything that can be used to filter you out of an interview. Never include anything that is not relevant. As you consider the following categories, and the kinds of information listed, constantly ask yourself, "Is this relevant to the kind of work that I am seeking?" Previous job applicants have been unsuccessful because their resumes failed them. A recent survey of employers revealed the following resume flaws:

1. No accomplishments (78 percent)
2. Negative visual impact (55 percent)
3. Poor or no cover letter (40 percent)
4. Lack of objective (36 percent)
5. Format problems (32 percent)
6. Irrelevant data (29 percent)
7. Inadequate job description (12 percent)
8. Unexplained time gaps (10 percent)
9. Resume too long (10 percent)[2]

Keep these items in mind as you read about resumes and their important sections.

Important Resume Sections

Identification
This is the place for your name, address with Zip code (permanent and local address if applicable), your telephone and fax numbers with an area code, and your e-mail address. Do not list your cell phone number, and make sure that the outgoing message on your answering machine is professional.

Objective
An objective states which job you have targeted and what you can do. It can be as simple as the title of the position you are applying for, or as persuasive as describing how you will benefit the employer. Normally an objective will cover five areas:

- **Functional interest area** (marketing, information technology, research)
- **Type of organization** (retailing, bank, nonprofit association, manufacturing)
- **Level of position** (entry level, lateral move, advanced level)
- **Future goals** (aspirations for movement in next few years)
- **Size, scope, location of organization** (small, large, local, regional, national, international)

Word your job objective in terms of the employment needs at the organization you are contacting. If you are simultaneously applying for an administrative position with a health organization and for a management training program with a corporate bank, your objective will differ significantly. In that case create two resumes, each with a different and specific objective. This will give a clear impression that you understand the job you are seeking, and that you desire to do that work for the company. You can also explain the difference in your cover letter. Table 2.2 lists some sample career objectives.

Table 2.2 Sample Career Objectives

Position

- Interested in joining a market research firm or a market research department as an analyst. Long-term goal is a senior management position in research.
- Desire position as copywriter for public relations firm, advertising agency, or in-house marketing department.
- Interested in entry-level buying position with large department store, leading to management responsibilities.
- Seeking position as a community health director for a town or city in the Southwest.
- Wish to begin a career as a programmer or systems analyst using my quantitative and mathematical training.
- Seeking a summer internship as an analyst's assistant in a large New York City investment company.

Field

- Desire opportunity with public relations staff of large organization. Qualified in photography, copywriting, editing, preparing news releases, and working articles for company publications.
- Interested in bank-management training program with emphasis on finance.
- Desire entry-level position in bank branch management, credit analysis, or commercial and installment lending area.
- Wish to work in human-resource area of a government agency in an entry-level position.
- Would like to work for a chemical, pharmaceutical, petroleum, or electronics firm, in the area of marketing or sales, utilizing my technical background in physics, chemistry, and biological sciences.
- Interested in production phase of manufacturing, including production scheduling, first-line supervision, inventory control, purchasing, quality control or industrial engineering.
- Wish to begin career in media or market research department with large agency. Eventual goal is account executive position.

Skills

- Seeking position utilizing strong research and writing skills. Particular interest in public relations or publishing. Examples of work are available.
- Seeking position utilizing supervisory experience and strong organizational skills. Specific interest in management training programs with retailing firm.
- Desire a position utilizing organizational, interpersonal, and communication skills. Particular interest is in production or operations management.
- Seeking a position that will utilize my strong quantitative, math, and communication skills. Particular areas of interest are data processing and research.

Source: Adapted from Career Objectives. Publication of Career Services, College of Agricultural and Life Sciences, University of Wisconsin–Madison (pp. 2–4). Retrieved September 21, 2002, at **http://www.cals.wisc.edu/students/cscaro.html**; Sample Career Objectives. Publication of Marquette University (pp. 1–3). Retrieved September 21, 2002, at **http://www.marquette.edu/csc/pages/JobHuntGuide/samples.htm**; Sample Career Objectives and Summary Statements. Rutgers University (2 pp.). Retrieved September 21, 2002, at **http://www.rutgers.placementmanual.com/resume/resume-02.html**.

Avoid trite, overused comments like: "Desire a challenging position with a rapidly growing firm, offering training and advancement." Employers ignore applicants that are passively looking for "any job," and are attracted to those that have something to offer them. Your objective should be work- and employer-centered, not self-centered.

In writing an objective, candidates often develop the statement around one of three themes: position, field, or skill. Sample statements would then look like these:

- **Position:** "Seeking a position as a financial analyst. . . ."
- **Field:** "Seeking an internship in the health care field. . . ."
- **Skills:** "Seeking a position where I can utilize my sales and speaking skills. . . ."

The problem with the use of a single theme is that it limits the overall scope and it focuses on you and not the employer. It is better to name the position you want, list some skills, and name the setting. This objective is much improved: "Desire to contribute strong _____ skills for the _____ company through proven experience in a _____ capacity." While you should describe a specific job, functional fields, or a type of industry, do not list two unrelated fields, such as real estate and banking. That can make you appear indecisive.

There is also a negative to consider in listing a job objective. It can take up valuable space, it is sometimes expressed too broadly, or it can limit you in being interviewed for a particular job—especially if the recruiter does not need your skills at that time.

Summary Statement

Individuals who are several years removed from their college experience often use a summary statement in place of the job objective. In this statement you can list your title, years of experience, special skills, and character traits that encapsulate your best qualifications and selling points. A short summary is an ideal place to list skills like computer abilities or foreign-language fluencies. Since this is a summary, it should be no longer than two or three sentences.

Here is an example of a summary statement: "CPA with twelve years experience with two Fortune 100 companies. Technical skills include P & L, budgeting, forecasting, and variance reporting. Bilingual fluency in Spanish and English was used in managing a diverse group of subordinates. A creative self-starter; each project was approached in an analytically detailed and thorough manner. My work contributed to ten straight years of record profits."

Education

If you are still in school, or have just graduated from college, this is the next entry. However, if you have had extensive work experience in the field for which you are applying, put the "Experience" section before "Education." List your degrees and graduation dates (or projected graduation date) in reverse-chronological order, starting with the most recent colleges; list only those from which you earned degrees. Omit high schools.

Include majors, minors, and concentrations in your description. You can highlight significant courses; if they are unusual, or you have little else to list, add a description of any significant research papers or reports, or list the skills and knowledge acquired in a course. List your grade-point average (overall or major) and class standing only if they are exceptional. You can also add academic honors or awards that are related to the degrees. Or, if you have received several awards you can list them in a separate section.

Experience
This section can carry one of several titles: "Experience," "Work History," or "Employment." When describing your work include the company name and location with city and state, your job title, the dates of employment, description of responsibilities, and major achievements. Start with your most recent position and work backward. Achievements look best in bulleted form. Be honest and factual, but emphasize the more-important positions, and minimize the less important.

Include both your duties and your accomplishments. **Duties** indicate what you have done in the past, and tell an employer what you can do for the company. **Accomplishments** tell how you have gone above and beyond the required duties. Duties sound basic and bland: "wrote reports," "researched issues," and "stocked product lines." When you add accomplishments your resume suddenly shines and can set you apart from others: "Wrote weekly reports for top management that summarized the sales demographics of four different divisions." "Was chosen to research mutual-fund load issues and created an archival database that saved the firm's brokers several hours weekly." Accomplishments must be believable and verifiable. You may prefer to cluster experiences into general categories like: "Related Experiences," "Professional Experience," or "Relevant Experience."

Remember, this section should be accomplishment-oriented and not duty- or responsibility-driven. State the number of people supervised, amount of budget controlled, and special projects. Table 2.3 describes the top twelve accomplishments that most interest employers.

If you have trouble remembering accomplishments, review the notes you made in Chapter 1, and consider your answers to the following questions:

- In each job, what special things did you do that set you apart?
- How did you make the job your own?
- In what ways did you take initiative?
- Were you promoted? If so, what special things contributed?
- Did you leave the company and its people better off as a result of your efforts?
- Did you win any awards or receive letters of praise?
- What are you most proud of in each job?
- How can you quantify what you accomplished?

If you have limited work experience, include summer and part-time employment along with internships, co-op positions, work-study, practicums, and even volunteer work. Identify in this section any specific skills or credentials that are related to your job objective. Do not mention salary.

Table 2.3 Top-Twelve Job Accomplishments Desired by Employers

- Increased revenues
- Saved money
- Increased efficiency
- Cut overhead
- Increased sales
- Increased workplace safety
- Purchasing accomplishments
- New products/new lines
- Improved record-keeping process
- Increased productivity
- Successful advertising campaign
- Effective budgeting

Source: Adapted from Resume Tips. S.C. Riverside: Search & Recruitment Specialists to the Collection Industry (4 pp.). Retrieved September 22, 2002, at **http://www.scriverside.com/pages/rtips.php**.

As you complete the experience section keep the following suggestions in mind:

- Be action-oriented. Use strong **action verbs** to describe your accomplishments. Describe and explain what the experiences were rather than when and where they occurred. Table 2.4 displays a list of active verbs that you can borrow from. They are divided into a variety of skill areas.
- Use nouns that convey key skills or knowledge. Examples include: organized IT projects using C++, completed monthly projects using Excel, and developed a new sales route in Southern California because of fluency in Spanish.
- Keep personal pronouns out of the descriptions.
- Quantify your accomplishments whenever possible to show the scope of your responsibilities. ("Managed a team of five engineers" or "Administered a budget of $500,000.")
- Don't list reasons for leaving previous employers. Such statements are open to misinterpretation and assumptions. This information is best discussed during the interview.

Volunteer/Community/or Extra-Curricular Activities
If your work experience is insufficient to stand alone, and you have had other significant work activity, list the nonwork responsibilities you held and the learning that you obtained. It is especially important to note any leadership positions, committees you served on, or activities you organized. But make sure the items listed really support the job you are seeking. Some employers may not see your church activities or Rotary Club office as valuable to them or as evidence of leadership, especially if the overall focus of your extracurricular activities is narrow.

Table 2.4 Action Verbs for Resume Use

Management Skills
administered
analyzed
assigned
attained
chaired
consolidated
contracted
coordinated
delegated
developed
directed
evaluated
executed
improved
increased
organized
oversaw
planned
prioritized
produced
recommended
reviewed
scheduled
strengthened
supervised

Technical Skills
assembled
built
calculated
computed
designed
devised
engineered
fabricated
maintained
operated
overhauled
programmed
remodeled
repaired
solved
upgraded

Communication Skills
addressed
arbitrated
authored
collaborated
convinced
corresponded
developed
directed
drafted
edited
enlisted
formulated
influenced
interpreted
lectured
mediated
moderated
negotiated
persuaded
promoted
reconciled
recruited
spoke
translated
wrote

Public Relations
advertised
advocated
attended
coordinated
convinced
dispensed
disseminated
distributed
fundraised
handled
influenced
lobbied
persuaded
publicized
recruited
screened
serviced
targeted

Financial Skills
administered
allocated
analyzed
appraised
audited
balanced
budgeted
calculated
computed
developed
forecasted
managed
marketed
planned
projected

Research Skills
abstracted
clarified
collected
critiqued
diagnosed
evaluated
examined
extracted
identified
inspected
interpreted
interviewed

Table 2.4 Action Verbs for Resume Use (concluded)

investigated	established	classified
organized	fashioned	collected
researched	founded	compiled
reviewed	illustrated	dispatched
summarized	initiated	executed
surveyed	instituted	generated
systematized	integrated	implemented
	introduced	inspected
Teaching Skills	invented	monitored
advised	originated	operated
adapted	performed	organized
clarified	planned	prepared
coached	revitalized	processed
communicated	shaped	purchased
counseled		recorded
demonstrated	**Helping Skills**	retrieved
demystified	assessed	screened
developed	assisted	specified
enabled	clarified	systematized
encouraged	coached	tabulated
evaluated	counseled	validated
explained	demonstrated	
facilitated	diagnosed	**More Verbs for Accomplishments**
informed	educated	achieved
instructed	expedited	expanded
persuaded	facilitated	improved
set goals	familiarized	pioneered
stimulated	guided	reduced (losses)
trained	motivated	resolved (problems)
	referred	restored
Creative Skills	rehabilitated	spearheaded
acted	represented	transformed
conceptualized		
customized	**Clerical/Detail Skills**	
designed	approved	
developed	arranged	
directed	catalogued	

Source: Adapted from: "Resume Writing: Action Verbs." Hegi Family Career Development Center, Southern Methodist University. Retrieved September 22, 2002, at http://www.smu.edu/career/careersmu/resume_guide/action_verbs.html; "Action Verbs for Your Resume." The Liberal Arts Career Services, The University of Texas at Austin. Retrieved September 18, 2002, at http://www.lacs.utexas.edu/student/resume_verbs.html; "The Resume: Action Words." St. Vincent College. Retrieved September 22, 2002, at http://www.stvincent.edu/services/career/resume/.

Honors

If you have enough honors or recognitions to stand alone, list them under a separate heading. Honor areas can include sports, community service, academic, and employment.

Military Service

If you served in the military, treat it as a continuation of your employment or experience section. List the branch, dates of service, your rank, and present obligation. Describe any military work assignments that relate to your present job objective. Mention your honorable discharge.

Personal Background

Here you can highlight interests, hobbies, language fluency, computer competency, publications, presentations, certifications, professional associations, significant international travel, and special honors and accomplishments if these were not listed in a separate area. Highlight leadership positions and both elected and nonelected offices. Be careful here. This section works well if you have done something unusual or have had little work experience. Nothing is gained, however, if you simply list tennis, skiing, and hanging out with friends.

References

This section refers to people who are in a position to describe you, and your achievements, characteristics, and your previous work record. Do not use names unless the people listed have expressly agreed to write a recommendation for you. Most job experts recommend that you make a list of the references on a separate sheet of paper and have it available. On your resume insert a statement like, "References are available upon request."

Three Kinds of Standard Resumes

The following section describes three kinds of standard resumes: chronological, functional, and skills emphasis. All three are print versions. Electronic and scannable resumes will be examined in Chapter 3. In addition, two special purpose resumes are described: combination chronological-functional and curriculum vitae. By examining a variety of different resumes, both traditional and online, you will see how each meets specific needs and describes individual accomplishments.

Each different resume type allows you to present yourself to different employers in different ways. That means that when you are looking for different types of jobs you may end up using a different resume for each. The **chronological** format may best facilitate the question-and-answer process in an interview. For showing that your abilities are exactly what a company needs for a specific job, the **skills emphasis** resume may be the best. Or the **functional** style may allow an employer to learn more about you than your previous work experience listing might show.

Chronological Resume

A chronological resume is commonly referred to as the traditional resume. It is easy to read because it lists your educational background and your work experience in reverse chronological order. It highlights job titles, company and school names, dates of enrollment and employment, responsibilities, and other pertinent information needed by the employer. All of this is described in detail.

A chronological resume works best if you have steady career growth, intend to remain with your current employer, are looking for a job in a company or profession directly related to the one you are presently in, or if your intended profession calls for it. Certain professions, such as education, law, and accounting, require a chronological resume. A chronological format also benefits those in the consulting, finance, and information technology fields.

If you can answer "yes" to the following questions, you should consider using a chronological resume:

- Can you show continuity in your work history?
- Are you looking for a job related to your past career experience?
- Are you unconcerned about employers seeing gaps in your past?
- Do you want to emphasize nonprofessional jobs that you have held?
- Does your job history show progress?
- Do you work in a field in which a traditional job-search method is used?
- Can someone look at your resume and know the job you are seeking without a stated career objective?

There are dangers in using a chronological format. Less-impressive jobs and titles are easily seen. Frequent job changes are apparent. Gaps between jobs are evident. Less-professional jobs (for example: summer or part-time work; or work as a clerk, server, construction worker, or office assistant) receive as much emphasis as professional jobs. These problems are especially disconcerting for people reentering the job market, for a graduate student with no work experience, and for the college student whose only work experience has been part-time and summer jobs in fast-food restaurants, at local supermarkets, as a lifeguard, or as a clerk in the family business. If you fall within one of these categories, read on, but also consider using a functional or skills emphasis resume, which will be described next.

In addition, a chronological resume places little value on unpaid work such as community programs, campus activities, and volunteer associations.

Figure 2.1 displays the resume of Geoffry Biggs. Geoffry is a college student who is looking for a summer internship in the fields of marketing and retail. He has had some good jobs, and he displays those very well in a traditional chronological form. Notice that the reversed dates are easily seen in the left margin.

Functional Resume

The functional resume is preferred to a chronological resume if there are gaps you do not want to emphasize, or if your background does not include the normal things that go into the chronological format (for example, work experience).

The functional resume does list your education and jobs, but it organizes this material in a more-concise way and allows your skills, abilities, or experiences to be described by activity instead of by employment history, job titles, company names, and dates of employment. You can describe the activities you have found most satisfying, what research you have done, and how you have handled problems or man-

Figure 2.1 Chronological Resume—Summer Internship

<u>Current Address:</u>
3809 Cobbler
St. Cloud, MN 56300
331-371-5555
gbigs@scsu.edu

<u>Permanent Address:</u>
7315 West 9th
St. Paul, MN 56315
910-777-1181

Geoffry Biggs

Objective	To obtain a summer intern position in Marketing or Retailing utilizing my organizational, communication, and leadership skills.
Education	**St. Cloud State University** St. Cloud, MN Bachelor of Business Administration, May 2004 Major: Marketing: Specialization in Retailing Overall GPA: 3.5/4.0 Financed 75% of education
Work Experience 05/02–08/02	**Dayton's Department Store** Minneapolis, MN *Infant's Merchandising Coordinator* • Developed, organized and maintained visual displays • Ensured appropriate stock levels • Provided reports to management
05/01–08/01	**Fingerhut Merchandising** St. Cloud, MN *Inventory Inspector* • Maintained proper merchandise level • Re-stocked return merchandise • Was introduced to catalogue business
04/00–10/00	**International House of Pancakes** St. Cloud, MN *Waiter* • Trained new waiters • Used interpersonal skills to serve customers quickly and efficiently • In charge of "take-out" section
Leadership Experience	Residence Hall Advisor (08/01–05/02) Marketing Club Vice-President Salvation Army Angel Tree Organizer

aged people. A functional format allows you to relate your past and your capabilities in an exciting, personal, and re-marketable way. You can even include travel, community activities, and sports. The functional resume is preferred to the traditional if:

- You are changing careers;
- You are entering the job market with no work history but have other relevant experience to offer;
- You have had diverse jobs and experiences that do not appear to combine into a viable career field;
- Your previous work has been temporary or freelance;
- You want to emphasize strengths that were not used in recent work experience;
- You are returning to the job market after an absence and with a gap in your work history;
- You are seeking a position unrelated to your previous employment;
- Your past career success has not been continuous and progressive;
- You have a lengthy employment history and want to direct an employer away from that history to focus on your strengths; and/or
- You are moving from one professional realm into another (for example, office assistant to manager).

Some functional activities that provide relevant experience include course work, internships, student government, volunteer work, extracurricular involvement, and military experience. A weakness of the functional resume is that some employers may be accustomed and partial to a chronological resume, with items listed in order.

In Figure 2.2 we see that John Espinoza's resume is designed to accomplish many of the above objectives. While it contains traces of a chronological design, the dates are more subtly contained within the education description, and the employment dates are listed at the end of the resume along with job responsibility. By using a functional approach John is stressing his work experience and not the place of work. He shows his educational and job achievements in a specific order. By doing this he is telling employers that he has moved from client, group, and casework through agency administration, and now with an MBA he is qualified and ready to direct an organization.

Rhiannon Woo's resume (Figure 2.3) also takes a functional approach. Rhiannon desires to work in an international field, so she stresses her coursework and related experiences.

Combination Chronological-Functional Resume

Since a need often exists between listing some items chronologically and freely describing other areas, a growing trend has emerged between combining segments from both the chronological and functional resumes. You can put sections like work history and education in a reverse-chronological sequence. Some candidates even box off those portions of their resume. You can cluster the rest of your material in a functional manner using headings such as "Areas of Effectiveness," "Qualifications," or "Summary."

Figure 2.2 A Functional Resume

John T. Espinoza
1125 Bennet Way
San Jose, California

(408) 555-4360 (home)
(408) 555-0157 (work)
(408) 555-3298 (fax)

OBJECTIVE: Seek directorship of community-based social organization.

EDUCATION: Master of Business Administration, May 2003
University of California, Berkeley, California
Master of Social Work, May 2001
San Jose State University, San Jose, California
Thesis: "Effective Design of Community-Based Programs for Juveniles in Santa Clara County." A comprehensive survey of junior and senior high students and community program administrators to determine effectiveness of community-based adolescent programs.
Bachelor of Arts in Social Services, May 1995
University of the Pacific, Stockton, California
Able to read, write, and speak Spanish fluently.

EXPERIENCE:
Casework
Coordinator and Counselor for community-based agencies, experienced in assessing immediate and long-range needs of families in a variety of stress areas including marital discord, delinquency, drug abuse and unemployment. Interacted with clients both individually and in groups, making referrals to service agencies as needed. Initiated individual follow-up and reevaluation procedures.

Group Work
Created, organized, and supervised after-school and weekend recreational programs for adolescents. Designed and implemented local ongoing basketball competition program as a major group fund-raising event. Co-facilitated parent group counseling sessions on teenage drug abuse.

Administration
Organized, trained, and supervised group of volunteers for operation of stress hotline program; wrote and was awarded grant for development of a social service handbook. Coordinated the research and publishing of *Directory of Community Services* currently in use by American Red Cross, YMCA, and Santa Clara County Department of Social Services.

AFFILIATIONS: Member of National Association of Social Workers, 1995–Present. President of Undergraduate School of Social Work Organization at University of Pacific, 1994–1995. Publicity Chairperson of Cinco de Mayo Festival, City of Stockton, 1996.

EMPLOYMENT: GROUP COUNSELOR MANAGER/COORDINATOR
(field work practicum), 2001–2003
Salvation Army-San Jose Community Center
San Jose, California

COUNSELOR, 1999–2001
Family Service Association of the Mid-Peninsula
1103 Carmel Avenue
Palo Alto, California

COORDINATOR, 1996–1998
Big Brothers Agency of San Joaquin County
Stockton, California

Figure 2.3 A Functional Resume (Recent College Graduate)

Rhiannon Woo
123 Baseline
Boulder, CO 23920
(310) 850-7321

Career Focus: International Trade in the Pacific Rim

Education
    University of Colorado, Boulder, Colorado

    B.S., Business Administration (2003)
    Emphasis: **International Business**

Representative Coursework

Intro to International Business	International Finance
Management of Multinational Enterprises	International Marketing
World Commerce and Development	International Management

Related Experiences
- **Pacific Rim Trip:** Visited Hong Kong, Bangkok, Thailand, Seoul, and Singapore in connection with CU coursework. Opportunity gave exposure to conducting business in the Pacific Rim.
- **International Business Internship:** Under direction of CU Small Business Center, worked with entrepreneurs from Ireland in researching, identifying, and contacting companies offering potential for import/export business.
- **Import Experience:** Presently employed with Far East Trade Company which specializes in importing fine jewelry from Hong Kong, Malaysia, and India; recommend product purchase, maintain inventory, and organize shows for sales in five western states.

Computer Usage
    Extensive computer coursework (60+ hours) with knowledge of various desktop hardware and software applications, including Lotus 1-2-3, Microsoft Office, and dBase III+ and IV. Extensive World Wide Web application with use of selected international databases.

Employment Summary
    Personally financed 100% of education through the following employment:

Import/Sales: Far East Trade Company	2001–Present
Assistant Manager/Driver: Boulder Cab	2000–2001
Convention Coordinator: Broker Hotel	1999–2000
Waiter: Bouldrado Hotel	1998–1999

Affiliations
    International Business Association
    Pacific Rim Trade Association
    Toastmasters International

Desire to Relocate—References Upon Request

The combination approach allows you to be creative. You can describe how as a residence-hall advisor you reacted to disruptive behavior on your hall floor; how you tied together the material learned in two or three classes to produce a significant research project; how your professor incorporated your research in a paper; how you established and managed a housepainting company in the summers of your college years and sold it upon graduation; or how your quick reaction saved a drowning child at the swimming pool.

If you have been working for several years, you may be leery of using a totally functional style. Some human resource departments and employment agencies frown on its use, and a large percentage of the resumes in the marketplace seem to be chronological. Nevertheless, your resume works as an intended marketing tool if it gets people to see you—and believe in you—in a way they otherwise would not. If your resume looks like 2,000 other resumes, all traditional, how is an employer going to pull yours from the pile in order to grant the interview? You have to choose what puts you in the best light. A combination functional and chronological approach may be the answer.

Skills Emphasis Resume

A skills emphasis resume resembles a functional resume in format. It always leads off with the identification section followed by an objective or desired position. The objective should highlight some of the skills that you will describe in your resume. For example, "Desired: A SALES POSITION leading to a career in staff marketing and management where I can use my skills of leadership, communication, financial analysis, and creativity." Next, include a short personal-background narrative, then a description of how your background has helped you develop various skills, such as leadership, communication, analysis, or creativity.

At this point you may want to refer back to Chapter 1 and the discussion on transferable skills. These are skills that you have developed from a variety of sources, such as past work experience, volunteer activities, classroom assignments, community participation, and hobbies. Some sample skill headings are listed in Table 2.5. Consider those that fit you the best. Consider also the skills that are required in the particular job you are applying for and by the company you desire to interview with.

Under the headings you will list information about your work experience, education, or other activities that will illustrate and support your skills.

Figure 2.4 displays the skills emphasis resume of Sarah Dunn. Sarah's career objective is for a job in which four of her specific skills can be used. She displays how she has developed those skills through a listing of professional accomplishments.

Each of the three resume types serves a specific purpose. As your jobs change, as you complete educational programs, or as you develop new skills, you will often find it necessary to change your resume style. Figures 2.5 and 2.6 show how this can be done.

Deborah Moore started her career as a sales representative. Slowly she moved into procurement and finally held two positions as a senior buyer. For years her chronological resume served her well. But after finishing an Executive MBA program she is repositioning herself for a Chief Financial Officer position. Consequently, a skills emphasis resume better suits her needs. The change is shown in Figure 2.6.

Table 2.5 Skill-Description List

Accounting	Fund Raising	Project Management
Administrative	Instructional	Public Relations
Advertising	Interpersonal	Public Speaking
Analytical	Interviewing	Quantitative
Budgeting	Laboratory	Research
Coaching	Leadership	Sales
Communication	Listening	Supervisory
Computer	Managerial	Teaching
Consulting	Meeting Deadlines	Teamwork
Coordinating	Motivation	Technical
Counseling	Multicultural	Telemarketing
Creative	Multimedia	Telephone Solicitation
Customer Service	Negotiation	Training
Data Collection	Organizational	Writing
Decision Making	Persuasion	
Editing	Physical Dexterity	
Entrepreneurial	Planning	
Financial Development	Presenting	
Foreign Language	Problem Solving	

Curriculum Vitae (CV)

This final resume style is not considered one of the standard resumes, for it is used primarily by individuals in academic and research fields. The **curriculum vitae** is also called a **CV** or **vita**. The one-page minimum standard for business resumes does not apply for CVs, because applicants try to give potential employers a totally thorough picture of who they are and what they have done.

Instead of following a standard CV format, candidates normally confer with colleagues and mentors regarding the style to use in particular fields. However, some typical categories can be identified. Table 2.6 displays some of those categories.

Constructing Your Resume

Organizing the Resume Content

Organize and focus your resume. Don't follow a free-flow form of writing, listing things helter-skelter. Organize your message into a simple, complete, and concise outline. A journalistic approach helps here. Reporters start their story with a headline and a leading paragraph that captures the reader's attention and gives the basic information needed to understand the story that follows. Each major division and subdivision of your resume should lead with a headline, contain an excellently worded

Figure 2.4 A Skills Emphasis Resume

SARAH DUNN
1234 Harvest Avenue
Atlanta, Georgia 49532

Work (422)555-3567
Home (422)555-7654

CAREER OBJECTIVE

MARKETING SUPPORT REPRESENTATIVE where skills in administration and management, program development, public relations, and writing can be used.

PROFESSIONAL ACCOMPLISHMENTS

Administrative/Management
- Selected and trained sales and volunteer staffs of up to twenty individuals.
- Managed and authorized expenditures of budgets exceeding $600,000.
- Received "State Award for High Achievement in Health Field."

Program Development
- Created innovative public health education and patient services programs for three counties.
- Raised over $150,000 for American Heart Association through "Run-for-Life" program.

Public Relations
- Engineered sales achievement campaigns netting increased revenues of $75,000 in two months.
- Designed marketing-oriented brochures, posters, and fliers for numerous organizations.

Writing/Editing
- Served as editor of community health newsletter with a circulation of 20,000.
- Authored *Training Manual for Volunteer Health Educators*.
- Researched and was awarded grants totaling over $50,000.

EXPERIENCE SUMMARY

Assistant Director, American Heart Association, Atlanta. Initiated and developed tri-county programs for community education. Developed and implemented budgets. Wrote several grants for additional funding of programs. Administered extensive community education projects. (May 2002–present)

Advisor, Academic Advisement Center, University of Georgia, Athens, Georgia. Counseled and advised diverse populations on academic concerns. Set up peer counseling program. Developed ongoing training program for volunteer staff. (Sept. 2000–May 2002)

Sales Supervisor, Neiman Marcus Department Store, Sunnyvale, California. Supervised four departments, twenty full and part-time salespersons. Trained all new personnel. Completed weekly sales progress reports. (June 1999–May 2000)

EDUCATION

Master of Business Administration (May 2002)
University of Georgia, Athens, Georgia

Bachelor of Arts Degree in Psychology (May 1999)
Tulane University, New Orleans, Louisiana

Figure 2.5 A Chronological Resume

Deborah Moore
129 Main Oak #27
Plano, Texas 75243
214-555-3125

EDUCATION:

2000–2003   *Southern Methodist University, Dallas, Texas*
Executive MBA—Finance concentration, August, 2003

1987–1991   *Miami University, Oxford, Ohio*
BBA—Marketing/Psychology, June 1991

WORK EXPERIENCE:

2000–Present   *Frito-Lay, Inc.—Plano, Texas*
Senior Buyer—Capital Equipment
Negotiated, prepared, and administered major domestic and international capital equipment contracts for new plant construction and companywide production innovations. Procurement project coordinator for Engineering and Research divisions. Total budget: $150 million.

1996–2000   *Quality Chemical Corporation—Dallas, Texas and Cleveland, Ohio*
Senior Buyer—Chemicals
Responsible for procurement of bulk commodities and specialty chemicals for Electrochemical, Soda Products, and Plastics divisions. Transportation interface included truck, rail, barge, and ocean vessel movements. Total budget: $60 million.

Buyer—Chemicals
Procurement of bulk commodities and minor metals for Electrochemical and Soda Products divisions. Total budget: $25 million.

1993–1996   *Arthur G. McKee Corporation—Cleveland, Ohio*
Purchasing Agent
Responsible for total instrumentation and control panel procurement for petrochemical contracts.

Administrative Assistant to Project Purchasing Manager
Assisted in the coordination of total procurement for domestic iron and steel and petrochemical projects.

Assistant Chief Expeditor
Supervised fourteen Assistant Buyers and In-Plant Expeditors.

Assistant Buyer
Expedited U.S. capital equipment for the construction of a Brazilian steel mill.

1991–1993   *Proctor & Gamble, Health & Beauty Aids Division—New Orleans, Louisiana*
Sales Representative for wholesale grocery, drug, variety, and mass-merchandise outlets in Louisiana and Mississippi with responsibility for complete merchandising and advertising programs. Winner of three first-place awards for direct shipment contests.

ADDITIONAL EDUCATION AND ACTIVITIES
ISO 9000 Compliance Seminar, Karass Negotiating Seminar, Kepner-Tregoe Problem Solving/Decision Analysis, Total Quality Management Training, Phases I and II, Juran Institute, Purchasing Management Association, Career-Track Seminar: "High Impact Communication Skills," "Personal Power for Unlimited Success" with Tony Robbins, "Completeness: Managing for The 21st Century" with Phillip Crosby

Figure 2.6 A Functional Resume (Recent College Graduate)

Deborah Moore
129 Main Oak #27
Dallas, Texas 75243
214-555-3125

DESIRE

A FINANCIAL MANAGEMENT POSITION, leading to a Chief Financial Officer position, that requires skills in negotiation, communication, financial analysis, planning, budgeting, and leadership.

Background includes: negotiating major domestic and international capital equipment contracts; individual and group presentation training and experience; contract financial background supplemented by MBA finance emphasis; contract renewal, inventory, and standard cost planning and budgeting skills; direct supervisory experience; knowledge of various skill seminar training techniques.

RELATED EXPERIENCE AND ACCOMPLISHMENTS

NEGOTIATION As a chemical and equipment senior buyer, led many successful individual and team negotiations for multimillion dollar contracts, resulting in outstanding cost savings.
When buying feedstock chemicals, completed purchasing negotiation seminar led by leading consultant in field.

COMMUNICATION As a sales representative, have had professional training and experience in making presentations. While working as a chemical buyer, further developed skills through quarterly presentations to upper management. Past performance reviews have favorably rated oral and written communication abilities.

FINANCIAL ANALYSIS Previous purchasing positions strengthened numerical analysis skills. As a graduate student, MBA courses were taken in Advanced Finance, International Finance, and financial intermediaries. Through employment as a senior capital equipment buyer, gained experience in the use of a personal computer and various financial software packages.

PLANNING AND BUDGETING After attaining the position of senior buyer, administered $60- to $150-million-per-year procurement budgets; successfully managed time, money, and human-resource constraints.

LEADERSHIP As a sales representative, won three volume sales contests. Throughout career have shown rapid progression from associate to senior buyer. With all employers, developed direct supervisory experience over buyers and expeditors. While working as a graduate assistant, wrote portions of a management text teaching manual.

WORK HISTORY

Senior Buyer, Frito-Lay, Inc., Dallas, TX. Contracted capital equipment for new plant construction from 2000 to present.

Senior Buyer/Buyer, Quality Chemical Corp., Dallas, TX, and Cleveland, OH. Purchased commodity chemical feedstocks, 1996-2000.

Purchasing Agent/Assistant Chief Expeditor/Assistant Buyer, Arthur G. McKee Corporation, Cleveland, OH. International capital equipment procurement experience in petrochemical and iron and steel industries, 1993–1996.

Sales Representative, Procter & Gamble Distributing Co., New Orleans, LA, 1991–1993.

EDUCATION

Executive MBA, Southern Methodist University, Dallas, TX, August 2003. Concentration in Finance.
BBA, Miami University, Oxford, OH, June 1991. Business studies in Psychology and Marketing.

Table 2.6 Sample Curriculum Vitae (CV) Headings

Personal Information
- Name
- Address
- Phone numbers
- E-mail
- Web page

Objective

Education/Preparation/Background
- Postgraduate work
- Graduate degree(s), major/minors, thesis/dissertation titles, honors
- Undergraduate degree(s), major/minors, honors

Professional Licenses/Certifications

Academic/Teaching/Employment/Experience
- Courses taught/developed/introduced
- Innovation in teaching
- Teaching evaluations

Administrative Experience

Technical and Specialized Skills

Research Skills

Other Related Experience

Professional/Academic Honors and Awards

Professional Development
- Conferences/workshops attended
- Other activities

Research/Scholarly Activities
- Journal articles
- Conference proceedings
- Books
- Chapters in books
- Magazine articles
- Papers presented/workshops/conferences
- Technical reports
- Work currently under review
- Work in preparation

Current Research Interest

Grants Received

Service
- Academic
- Professional
- Community

(continued on next page)

Table 2.6 Sample Curriculum Vitae (CV) Headings (concluded)

Professional Affiliations/Memberships
Foreign Language Abilities/Skills
Consulting
Volunteer Work
Honors and Awards
References

---

and focused lead paragraph, and complete the unit of thought with the remaining words. Short action-oriented phrases are used instead of complete sentences. A bulleted style of listing items makes the document more reader-friendly.

Follow the rules of good writing. Avoid using personal pronouns (I, my, me) and egotistical references. Use active rather than passive voice, and avoid jargon, clichés, and technical terms that can confuse. Try for originality in wording and never borrow phrases from other people's resumes.

A few years ago *The Wall Street Journal* assembled a group of recruiters who reviewed an executive resume and indicated how the wording either added or subtracted from the applicant's value to a company. The results can be viewed in Figure 2.7.[3]

Length of Resume

Does length matter? The norm for a resume is one page—but do not be persuaded to limit your resume to only one page if you truly need more space. Two or three pages are acceptable, *if your information is pertinent and necessary*. The key is to make sure everything you include is necessary. As you prepare the resume constantly ask yourself, Would shortening the document allow the same story to be told? The Harvard Graduate School of Business Administration several years ago laid down a general guideline for its graduates and alumni:

1 or 2 pages—for business school students with business experience
2 pages—for business school alumni up to ten years out
3 pages—for business school alumni more than ten years out.[4]

Often advanced students submit to the placement officer the requested one-page resume, and then later expand the one page into two or three pages. This is generally referred to as the **expanded data sheet**. The applicant carries the expanded form into the interview and can highlight new items for the interviewer.

Resume Appearance

Appearance is critical to making an immediately favorable impression. The resume should be inviting, easy to read, and should look professional. Make it easy to skim by emphasizing items with boldface, capitalization, underlining, or italics. It is even appropriate to use different font styles and sizes, but a font size of 10.5 or 11 is

Figure 2.7 The Value of Resume Wording

Pricing the Past

More than you may realize, your past is a price tag. What you've done, where you've lived and worked, the schools you've attended, even your hobbies—any and all of it can play into your pay. And those doing the playing and paying—recruiters and employers—are rarely more brutal than in tough times like these.

Here's how one professional might fare in the pricing game, based on suggestions from recruiters with an eye for detail—and a sharp pencil.

—*Gilbert Fuchsberg*

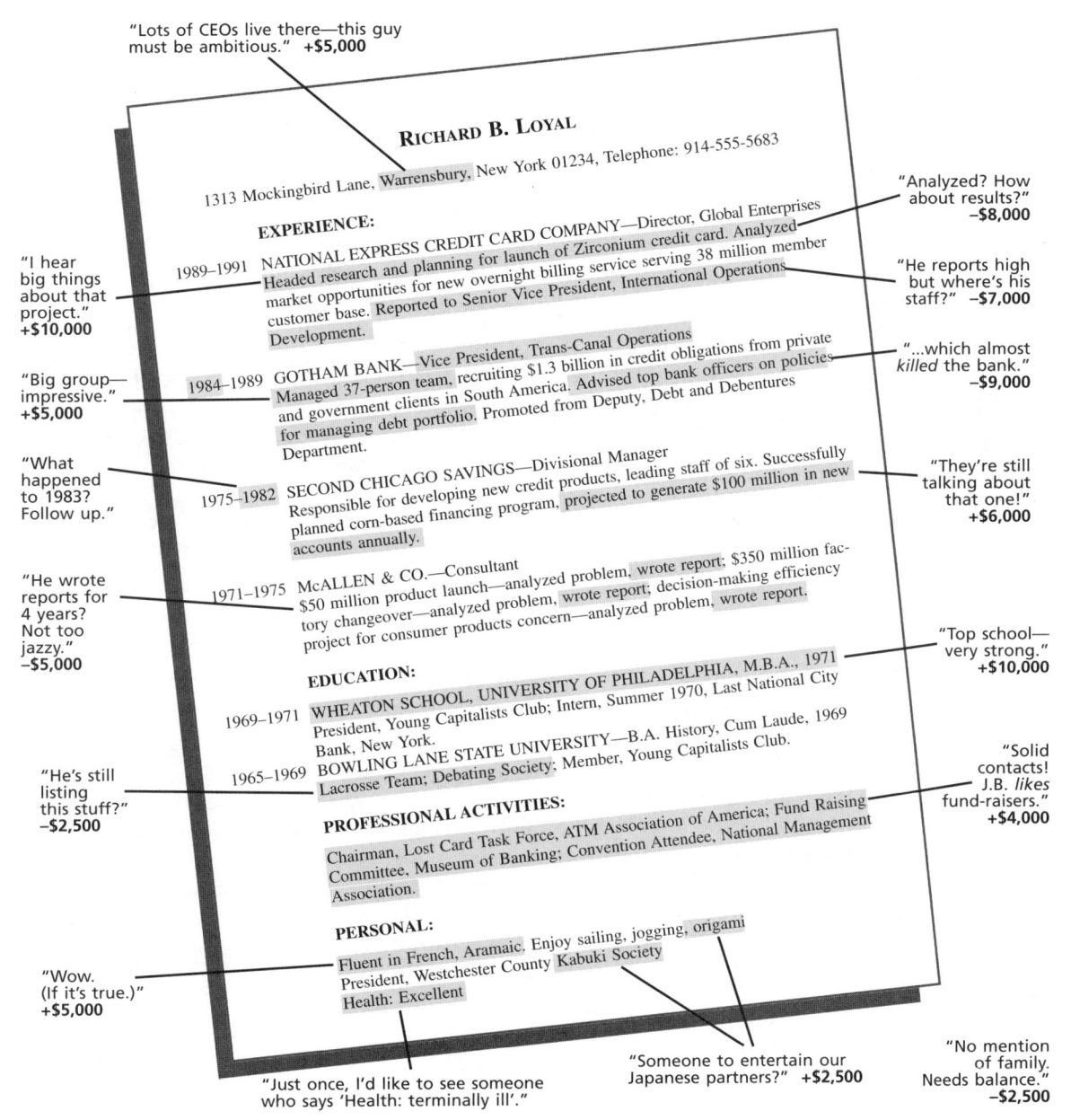

Constructing Your Resume

considered the minimum. Leave plenty of white space, especially between the separate sections and items listed. Proofread the document several times to assure that no typos, misspellings, or crossed-out information remain. Ask a trusted individual to also proofread it, and don't simply rely upon a computer spell-checker.

Make the final product crisp and clean. Use high-quality and heavy bond (20- to 24-pound) paper that matches the stationery and envelopes for your letters. For extra copies of your resume a high-quality laser paper will do. Avoid using colored paper that does not copy, fax, or scan well. The best colors are off-white, ivory, light tan, or light gray. Use a high-quality printer to ensure that the final copy reproduces well.

Save a few important items about yourself that are not placed in your resume. Since few people are hired from the reading of a resume, you should say what needs to be said and no more. Be honest, but never volunteer information that could preclude a face-to-face interview.

Resume Truthfulness

While resume puffery has always existed, and some people believe it is acceptable to lie on a resume, in reality it is costly. Recently there have been a long string of publicly known individuals who have lost career dreams and prestigious jobs because their resume proved to be inflated. The best advice is, Do not lie on your resume. Today the Internet makes it cheap and easy to run background checks. While you may never be caught, the use of small puffed-up facts can grow into the habit of falsifying more-important data. Once you are caught, your job will surely end, and with damaged credibility your professional life probably will be ruined.

A recent survey of 7,000 resumes by the executive-recruitment firm Christian & Timbers showed 23 percent of the executives misrepresented their accomplishments. What were the most frequent offenses? Misstating years on the job, achievements, inflated salaries, and omitted jobs.[5] A survey by computing service Automatic Data Processing (ADP), found more than 40 percent misrepresented their education and/or employment histories.

How should you avoid lying?

- Don't list jobs, titles, or accomplishments that you have never had.
- Don't list degrees that you have never earned.
- Don't call yourself a supervisor if you have never supervised.
- Don't state that you have had more job responsibility than you have actually had.
- Don't stretch facts in order to outsmart the interviewer. (A person making $50,000 says he is making $55,000 in hopes of pushing his new salary to $60,000.)

One college career center created a "quick test" for its students. Keep this in mind as you edit your resume to ensure it is honest and true. You should be able to answer "yes" to each of the following questions:

- Is it the truth?
- Are you proud of it?

- Are you willing to have an employer use the information to evaluate your candidacy, and later your promotions?
- Can you validate the statement through someone who knows you?[6]

Global Resume Characteristics

If you are interested in global work your resume must have an international focus. This means having some knowledge of the rules, customs, values, protocol, and business practices of the countries in which you are interested in working. The major sections of a standard resume that were listed at the beginning of this chapter are important in the United States—but that is not the case in all other countries. If you need a resume to send to another country, and do not know the format or items to include in the content, the use of a curriculum vita would be your best resource. Employers in most countries prefer the detailed information included in the CV.

Resumes in Great Britain and France resemble those from this country quite closely. They run one to two pages long and contain the identification information, objective, professional experience, education, and other activities. Military service and personal information is not included in England. In France an applicant must display a substantial job history. Application letters must accompany resumes in both countries.

In Germany a resume resembles a complete dossier of a candidate. Employers not only want to know your accomplishments, they want to be sure you are honest and accurate. Photocopies of diplomas, certificates, honors, and letters of recommendation must be included. Where personal information about family, religious affiliation, and the like is prohibited in the United States, it is desired in Germany. Application letters also accompany resumes in Germany, and should be very formal and usually two pages in length.[7]

Updating Your Resume

Update your resume every six months. This will make you more eligible for available promotions, allow you to list pertinent material while it is still fresh in your mind, and remind you to purge information as it becomes obsolete. For instance, by the time you are completing advanced work, you should no longer be listing the high school or prep school you attended. As you become established in your profession, limit your listing of college activities and substitute activities related to your job and post-college years.

Keep a file of information handy; put a reminder in the file each time you begin an activity or write something that is resume material. The accumulated notes will help you update your resume on short notice and remember all items of importance. Periodically this material can then be added to the resume file in your computer. It is a good idea to have an up-to-date resume available at all times.

Notes

1. *Student handbook on resume writing.* (p. 2). Boston, MA: Harvard Graduate School of Business and Administration.
2. Candidate services: Resumes. (n.d.). MRI Sales Consultants of Franklin County. Retrieved September 4, 2002, at **http://www.werecruit4u.com/candidate/resumes.htm**.
3. Fuchsberg, G. (1991, April 17). Pricing the past. *Wall Street Journal*, R3.
4. *Student handbook on resume writing*, p. 7.
5. Perotin, M.M. (2002, July 1). Fudging the facts. *The San Diego Union-Tribune*, E8.
6. Resume ethics. (n.d.). Bates College, OTC resume tutorial: Resume ethics and integrity. Retrieved September 6, 2002, at **http://abacus.bates.edu/career/help/tutorial/ethics.html**.
7. Chaney, L.H. (2000). *Intercultural Business Communication*, 2nd ed. (pp. 143–144). Upper Saddle River, NJ: Prentice Hall.

CHAPTER - 3

Electronic Resumes

As you conduct your job search you have probably seen statements like: "I Got My Job Online—and Soon So Will You," or "Enjoy Being Unemployed? Keep Job Hunting Online."[1] Such comments refer to how technology has changed the way people look for jobs. In Chapter 2 you examined the design and writing of standard paper resumes. In this chapter you will see how technology gives you another approach to career seeking: online job searches and the electronic resume.

Online Job Searching

Information technological change has allowed organizations to alter their former data collection process drastically. Today employers scan, download, upload, keyword search, and then bank thousands of resumes that they receive. All of this is done in a matter of minutes, saved on a small disk as compared to several file drawers, and never read by an individual.

For job seekers big changes have also occurred. The Internet gives job seekers access to vast amounts of information about vacancies and employers, 24-hour availability, broader geographic reach, networking, career development advice, and simplified resume distribution.[2] Consequently full-text, searchable online job and resume databases have grown quickly. Because of this change you can now use the growing web of computer networks to enhance your chances of getting the best job. Consider the following statistics:

- Over 100,000 sites offer resume posting and classified ad services.[3]
- By 2002, more than 52 million Americans had used the Internet to find job-related information.
- Over four million Americans go online daily to look for jobs.
- By age group, 61 percent of the Internet searchers are between 18 and 29, 42 percent are between 30 and 49, and 27 percent are between 50 and 64.
- A 2001 estimate of the number of resumes on the web was 20 million.[4]
- Men are twice as likely to look for jobs online.
- Job-type searches reveal that 50 percent of sales-related people look online, as do 44 percent of executives and professionals, and 49 percent of clerical and office workers.

- People in higher income brackets and with higher educational levels are more likely to search for jobs online.[5]
- Over 80 percent of recent college graduates have job-searched online.[6]

Do Companies Hire on the Internet?

Are companies really hiring online? As with most Internet statistics it is hard to really know. Research tells us that by April 2002, 91 percent of the Global 500 companies had a recruiting presence online. Broken down by region this showed 95 percent were American companies, 90 percent were Asia Pacific companies, and 92 percent were European-based companies.[7] It is estimated that by 2003 employers will spend $1.7 billion recruiting online.[8] Cisco Systems hires 66 percent of its staff via the Internet. But a Yankelovich poll showed that other companies hire only about 10 percent of their new employees online.[9]

While the verdict is still out on the success potential of being able to get a job through the Internet, as someone who is active in the job search, you should not totally discount this technological facility. It seems sure that the information technology movement will push all of us toward using the internet in the future—to either search for job information or to put our name into play for a possible job interview.[10]

The Internet will only be a help to job searchers who have a good understanding of their career desires and direction. If you are unsure about what you want to do, and of your skills and abilities, job-hunting on the Internet will be a major source of frustration. Before you spend time online, head over to your College Career Center or local job counselor for some clear advice on where to start.

Advantages of Online Job Searching

For individual companies the bottom line advantage is remarkable cost savings, closely followed by a steady flow of available talent. For example at Cisco Systems, 81 percent of the resumes received come via the web, 66 percent of new hires come from online recruiting, and 68 days are shaved off the company's hiring cycle by using this method. Another employer said the change makes great economic sense. The hiring cost of an employee goes from $12,000 for a classified newspaper ad, to $1,650 via the web.[11]

The traditional job search process and online searching are similar in that both require networking, preparing and sending resumes, interview preparation, and the sending of correspondence. According to job expert Richard Bolles, there are five primary uses of online services for job-hunting or career planning:

1. It is a place to post your *resume*;
2. It is a place for you to search for *vacancies*, listed by employers;
3. It is a place to get some job-hunting help or *career counseling*;
4. It is a place to find *information* about companies or organizations;
5. It is a place to make *contacts*, who may help you find information, or help you get an interview at a particular place.[12]

Dixon and Tiersten add four other advantages to Bolles's list:

1. *Global Availability.* For just a few dollars a month you can make contact with thousands of employers throughout the world and save thousands of dollars in travel expenses.
2. *Low Cost.* For just a few dollars you can reach thousands of potential employers at a fraction of the cost of printing and mailing resumes.
3. *Quick Access.* The real-time availability of discussion groups and referrals, and the ability to send your resume instantly and to answer employers' questions in turn, cuts your job-search time from days to minutes. You can be one of the first to apply for a job.
4. *Personality Tailoring.* With the exception of your creative writing style, the traditional job search approach requires you to wait until the interview to demonstrate your real personality. By going online, you increase your potential. This is especially true if you use the web, where you can add photos of yourself, audio snippets of your voice, and even video segments of your work and projects.[13]

Location of Online Job Searches

Richard Bolles, as described in Chapter 1, has become the fount of wisdom for job seekers. His *Parachute* book has become a primary source for how to find a job, and now his Web site is the first place to go online when you are job searching. **JobHuntersBible.com** is packed full of wonderful ideas about what you should do, and not do, in your search. Bolles provides links to a variety of job-listing sites. While you can use a regular Internet search engine to find different sites, Bolles's book and Web site highlight those he finds to be most valuable. Best of all, he constantly updates his site.[14]

According to three different research reports the current most popular web job sites are: **Hotjobs.com**, campus favorite **Monster.com**, **Jobs.com**, **CareerBuilder.com**, and **Dice.com**. Research also found that 76 percent of those who visited a top-ten career Web site in December 2001 logged on to just one site.[15] The web URLs for these and other databases are listed in Table 3.1.

You can find these Web sites and others by doing a quick online search. Before you invest a lot of time in that endeavor, though, read some disadvantages considered by Bolles.

Disadvantages of Online Job Searches

Richard Bolles found that the likelihood of obtaining a job when you send out a standard paper resume, without having a chance to interview, is one job for every 1,470 resumes sent. As you can see the odds are not too good—but he found the odds of obtaining a job online are even worse. In his research with the top-25 job sites, one famous resume site had 59,283 resumes posted, but in a 90-day period, only 1,366 employers looked at any of the resumes. Another site hosted 85,000 resumes and for the same period only 850 employers looked at them.[16]

Bolles gave the following reasons why so few job seekers find jobs online. For a resume to land a job seeker a job online, some employer "has got to be desperate . . .

Table 3.1 Online Job Hunter Service

Top Job Databases on the Web

Hundreds of employment sites list thousands of job advertisements. The following Web sites would be good places to look when searching for jobs.

1. Monster Board (www.monster.com)
Designed for a "younger" crowd, those below 35 years of age and still in the first ten years of their careers. Over a million resumes are posted with password-protection. Excellent set of references and career tools. Attracts over five million hits a month.

2. Career Builder (www.careerbuilder.com)
This job listing site is the result of a partnership of newspaper giants Gannett, Knight Ridder, and the Tribune Companies. Former job databases Career Path, Career Mosaic, and Head Hunter are now part of this organization. It combines employment opportunities of more than 130 local newspapers that reach more than 15 million weekly readers. Over 26 million visitors view the Web site each month.

3. America's Job Bank (www.jobsearch.org)
A predominately government site that gets its listings from state public employment agencies. Excellent selection of diverse jobs available. You can search by geographic location, education, salary, and/or experience.

4. Nation Job Network (www.nationjob.com)
This general job search engine lets you seek jobs or it will even e-mail you job possibilities. Searches can be done by career field, geographic region, education, or salary. A highlight is the special job databases.

5. Hot Jobs (www.hotjobs.com)
You can search by city, region, keywords, job type, and even international opportunities. Employers who use this site can create a "test manager" for specific openings. A "candidate manager" even sifts through resumes for organizations. This site is managed by Yahoo.

6. Net-Temps (www.net-temps.com)
This site is known as a giant for high-quality full- and part-time jobs. It has over 75,000 positions posted by over 1,500 firms. The listings are never more than 30 days old. Company personnel offices never get to review the resumes, only net-temp members who are third-party recruiters.

7. Dice.Com (www.dice.com)
A prime location for computer information technology professionals like programmers and system analysts. The problem with this site is that a searcher must go through a third-party recruiter.

8. Flip Dog (www.flipdog.com)
This database scours corporate Web sites for job listings. It boasts of over a half-million listings from 50,000 global employers. This presents a comprehensive way of looking for good jobs.

has got to go online . . . has got to stumble across the site . . . has got to accidentally stumble across your resume on that site . . . has got to take the time and trouble to read it . . . has got to take the time and trouble to print it out . . . [and] has got to decide, after studying it, that they like it enough to invite you in."[17]

Bolles surmises that the likelihood of getting a job online is less than two percent, unless you are in a select field. Over 20,000 different job titles exist in the job world. Of that enormous amount, 75 percent of the online job listings are for only seven job titles in the following fields: computers, engineering, electronics, technology, health care, financial, and academic fields.[18]

Electronic Resumes

The wise job hunter has two versions of a resume available: one is for a human reader and the other is for companies that use an electronic automated tracking system. The electronic version is called a scannable resume. You produce that version to send to employers who use Optical Character Recognition (OCR) software to scan your resume into their company resume databases. Experts estimate that 80 percent of resumes collected by both large and small companies end up being scanned. Some employers even search the databases of third-party Internet job-posting and resume-posting boards. However, you will never know if a company uses the OCR method unless you ask. Consequently it is wise to call a interviewer, recruiter, or company contact prior to mailing out your resumes to determine which type you should send.

Scannable Resume

The advantage to the scannable resume is that while a human reader may miss important details, a scanning system instantly searches key words that link your work history, title, years of experience, education, and skills to key words in the company's open positions. Your resume is then stored in the system, sometimes for years. Companies can scan hundreds of resumes in minutes.[19]

The limiting factor of using scannable resumes lies in the fact that your resume must be clear and concise in order to produce a "clean" image. While you can use your standard paper resume for this purpose, it is better to modify your document to ensure that it will match the capabilities of the company's database. One of the most critical modifications is to turn active verbs into key words.

Use Key Words

When people read traditional resumes they like to see action verbs. When computers read resumes they look for job-specific key words. These appear primarily as nouns or short phrases. These words describe the knowledge, skills, abilities, and experiences that a candidate possesses. In essence the words describe what you have done in the past, and thus, what qualifies you for the present job.

A company will have some key words that are mandatory and others that are desirable. For each job listing there will usually be 25 to 30 key words. A human reader decides these subjectively. When a match occurs between what the company wants and what you have, you score a "hit." You need to get as many hits as possible. Only resumes that contain mandatory key words survive. Resumes with the most mandatory key words will be the first selected by a human reader.

The selection of your resume can also be impacted by how close to the top of the page your key-word hits occur. For this reason it is advisable to create a **Key-Word Summary** that is placed near the top of your resume. A key-word summary is important even when you place key words throughout your resume. Search engines track the overall number of key words located in the resume. The outcome is called "key-word density," and is sometimes a deciding factor for the human reader.[20]

Common Key Words

These are the most common words used in a particular field or industry. You can familiarize yourself with the pertinent words by constantly browsing publications, newspapers, ads, and other online resumes. One of the first steps in making your resume scannable is to turn verbs into key words. The examples below show typical conversions.

Standard Functional Resume "I am a corporate safety analyst with a bachelor's degree in a related field. I have four years of experience in the field."

Scannable Resume "Corporate safety analyst. I have a Bachelor's degree (B.S.) in Chemical Engineering from the University of Michigan. Four years experience with OSHA regulations and ISO 9000 Certified."

Standard Functional Resume "I assisted the Marketing Director in creating a new marketing strategy for e-commerce."

Scannable Resume "Assistant creator of new e-commerce marketing strategy."

In the examples above the key words are "safety analyst," "chemical engineering," "OSHA," "ISO 9000" "Assistant," "Creator," "marketing strategy," and "e-commerce." In an online search, individual words are important and the correct placement of the words is just as critical for effectiveness and description. The computer does not care if you are "empowered," "directed," or "accomplished." It looks for the words it has been programmed to find.

Another example shows how you can use key words to tighten your career objective. You can get by with, "I want to be a computer systems engineer," in a standard paper resume. In an electronic resume the more specific the better: "Experienced IT manager, M.B.A., self-starter and team leader, designed data system and network configurations for UNIX 4.1.2, SOLARIS 1.2, and SYBASE Relational Database 4.9.2."[21]

Key words can be specific terms, buzzwords, jargon, trade terms, or even hard skills. You can use acronyms and abbreviations, but spell the words out as well. Other key words include "job titles, departments, key functions, relevant personality traits, computer hardware and software, programming languages, academic degrees, fields of study, [and] foreign languages, all relevant to the target job. These should be listed under common headings like: Objective, Experience, Employment, Appointments, Accomplishments, Education, Affiliations, Publications, Honors, and other appropriate terms."[22]

Key-Word Examples Look over the following examples of key words often programmed into searches.

Job Titles: Software Engineer, Purchasing Agent, Professor, Brand Manager, Chief Financial Officer.

Skills and Responsibilities: Systems Analysis, Application Tracking, Career Development, Market Research Strategic Planning, Environmental Scanning, New Product Design, Costing, Recruitment.

Acronyms and Industry Terminology: TCP/IP, C++, JAVA, RAD, Microsoft Excel, ADA, SWOT Analysis, GAAP, EEO Regulations, SEC Filings, RFP.

Education or Certification: Certified Network Administrator, MBA, MSA, CPA, Certified Public Accountant, ISO 9000.[23]

Avoid repeating key words. In most searches, each key word gets a primary count only once, regardless of how many times it is used. In the previous example, "OSHA" will only give one primary point—even if it is used 25 times. While 25 different uses would give you a high density count, it is better to increase the variety of words that you use instead of the number of times each word is used. Remember also to include key words in the cover letters that you send with your scannable resumes.

Steps in Creating a Key-Word Resume

You can determine your present key-word count by highlighting those words in your current paper resume. The number of highlighted words determines your current potential hits. Now try a synonym-creation exercise where you list similar words and their forms and tenses. Examples are the word "manage" (direct, conduct, control, guide, or supervise) or "procure" (procurement, procured, obtain, secure, acquire, gain, or earn). Add appropriate words from this list to your current key words. In addition to synonyms add industry acronyms and their properly spelled-out terms. Add any words you believe an employer would look for regarding job titles, skills, education, or industry. From the list that you have generated create your key-word summary.[24]

Basic Guide for Preparing a Scannable Resume

As you construct your scannable resume keep the following rules in mind.

1. Avoid using Microsoft Word resume templates. They do not scan well.
2. Keep the layout simple. Do not use graphics (art, shading, vertical lines). Avoid bullets, accent marks, and other forms of punctuation not normally found on the computer keyboard. In their place you can use asterisks (*), hyphens (-), or plus signs (+). Do not use tabs, italics, boldface, highlighting, or underlining. Use the space bar to indent.
3. Set margins so that text is no wider than 65 characters across the screen. Left-justify everything.
4. Place your name, alone and in capital letters, on the first line of the resume and on the first line of all following pages. Put your address and all phone numbers on separate lines below your name.
5. Capitalize all major headings and titles like JOB OBJECTIVE, WORK EXPERIENCE, EDUCATION, and related activities. While bold emphasis works with some systems it is best to stick with all capitals.
6. Personal data and reference statements should be omitted on scannable resumes.
7. Use common and easily recognizable fonts. Ideally sans serif works best (Helvetica or Arial). Common serif fonts like Times New Roman are also usable. Keep the font size between 10 and 14 points.

8. Single-space the content and do not condense spacing between letters or compress lines of text.
9. Correct all misspellings and typographical errors.
10. Print your resume on quality 8.5 by 11-inch white paper, using a laser or inkjet printer. Do not use a dot matrix printer.
11. While standard paper letters are normally limited to one page, your scannable resume can be longer if you have relevant information.
12. Do not fold or staple your resume. Mail your scannable resume along with a copy of your paper resume. Avoid faxing a scannable resume since many fax copies are not completely clear.[25] Figure 3.1 shows an example of an electronic resume.

E-mail Resume

Here is another standard resume that has been altered for sending by e-mail to an employer. After you have developed your scannable resume you will need to convert it to ensure that it can be read by everyone. You must prepare it in **ASCII Plain Text format.** You will generally use the e-mail version only if an employer requests that you submit it that way. An advantage of using this method is that it goes directly to the employer without being intercepted by the human resources department.

The biggest disadvantage is the way it looks: After having jazzed your paper resume with different fonts and specialty papers, it is hard to look at a plain text resume with admiration. Just keep the end result in mind: It is the content and the obtaining of an interview that really count.

How to Create an ASCII Resume

ASCII stands for American Standard Code for Information Interchange. ASCII text files are universal and can be read and displayed in different word-processing formats. This generic file contains just plain words. The characteristics removed are basically the same as those of the scannable resume: no pictures, special fonts, graphics, page numbers, or even boldface or italic highlighting. You can create an ASCII resume by taking one of your current resumes and then following the steps below. A sample ASCII resume is shown in Figure 3.2.

1. Take your current resume and change the font to 12-point Courier. Remove all graphics and features that are bold, italic, or underlined. Replace bullets with asterisks and hyphens. Use only the characters on your computer keyboard that are ASCII.
2. Remove your tabs and reset your margins so that 6.5 inches of text, or approximately 65 characters per line, will be displayed. This display is what most e-mail applications accommodate. Left-justify your text.
3. Run the spell-check on your resume.
4. Select this format to save your resume: "text only with line breaks."
5. Cut and paste your new ASCII resume into a plain-text editor such as Notepad or Simple Text. This will display your resume in ASCII format, just as it will look in an e-mail program.

Figure 3.1 A Scannable Resume

PAUL RIPLEY
P.O. Box 818
Oklahoma City, OK 73150
405-555-8765
pripley@aol.org

OBJECTIVE
Desire senior management human resource director position.

KEY-WORD SUMMARY
Human Resources Specialist, 10 years experience in personnel functions including management development, training, employee relations, benefits compensation, recruitment and outplacement. Certificate in ADA, Coaching, Negotiating, Myers-Briggs Type Assessment, and TQM Training. Specific training skills include Computer-Based, Interactive Video, Workplace Attitude, Diversity, Adult Learning, Needs Analysis, Teams Facilitation, and Group Facilitation.

PROFESSIONAL EXPERIENCE
GENERAL MOTORS ASSEMBLY PLANT, Oklahoma City, Oklahoma
Personnel Director, March 2000 to Present.
Direct report to Plant Manager, manufacturing facility with 2,500 employees.
Responsible for all corporate Human Resource related functions.
* Coordinate all recruiting, hiring, compensation management, employee benefits packages, and pension and insurance administration.
* Oversee labor/management/employee relations.
* Negotiated a four year labor contract that met corporate objectives.
* Reduced annual cost of Worker's Compensation Insurance and Group Health Plan by over 25%.
* Designed and implemented policies for Family & Medical Leave, Americans with Disabilities Act, Drug & Alcohol Abuse, and Sexual Harassment.

DELL COMPUTERS, Austin, Texas
Training Director, December 1996 to February 2000.
Reported to Vice President of Human Resources for computer manufacturing plant of 1,500 employees.
* Designed, developed, and delivered customized training that was determined by needs assessment.
* Coordinated all employee training, including vendor contracting for on-site programs.
* Reduced in-house cost of personal computer (PC) training by 27%.
* Designed database system for recording employee training records as part of ISO 9000 compliance.
* Provided company's highly popular diversity training program to 20 corporate clients.

Figure 3.1   A Scannable Resume (concluded)

PAUL RIPLEY
-2-

HALLMARK CORPORATION, Kansas City, Missouri
Human Resource Generalist, June 1994 to November 1996.
Reported to Human Resource Director for greeting card company with 2,000 employees.
* Successfully recruited artists, designers, programmers, and managers for corporate office.
* Wrote interviewing manual for supervisors and managers.
* Designed campus interview process for recruiters.

FRED PRYOR TRAINING, Kansas City, Kansas
Trainer, June 1992 to June 1994.
Reported to owner of pre-packaged seminar company.
* Initiated start-up functions for needs analysis and development of 25 client training programs.
* Created and developed 12 in-house training courses.
* Instructed five "public seminars" at sites across the nation and in Canada.
* Gained overview of training field through temporary assignments for several clients.
* Wrote copy for bi-monthly newsletter.

EDUCATION
Executive Master of Business Administration, concentration in Human Resources, 2003
University of Oklahoma, Norman, Oklahoma
Bachelor of Business Administration, 1994
University of Kansas, Lawrence, Kansas
Additional Professional Training
Human Resource Director Program, 2002
Harvard Business School, Boston, Massachusetts
Certificate in Human Relations, 2001
University of Oklahoma, Norman, Oklahoma

PROFESSIONAL ORGANIZATIONS
* American Society for Training & Development
* Human Resource Exchange
* Society for Human Resource Management
* Toastmaster's International

6. Check and proofread the new ASCII resume carefully since the reformatting often causes text problems to appear. This is also a good time to make a final change to any non-ASCII characters, which will show up as question marks, square blocks, or other junk characters.
7. Cut and paste your resume into an e-mail message to yourself for a final check before sending it to an employer.[26] Although it is possible to send your resume as an attachment, most employers' firewalls block attachments to prevent spamming, viruses, and other intrusions.

E-mail Cover Letter

A professional e-mail resume is always accompanied by a cover letter. The contents of the letter will be the same as those of a paper cover letter described in Chapter 4. You need to state who you are and why you are writing. Your subject line is a great place to creatively entice the reader to look at what you are sending. Using Paul Ripley's resume in Figure 3.1 as an example, an e-mail subject line could read: "Corporate experienced H.R. specialist for H.R. director position."

As you move to the opening paragraph, keep your creativity flowing. Hook the reader with your opening words and entice him or her to view your resume. Continuing the same resume example the opening of the first paragraph could state: "Your *Human Resource Training* magazine job position calls for an experienced Human Resources expert in recruiting, training, and benefits compensation. My ten years' experience with three major corporations has given me that experience, plus you would receive a specialist in needs analysis, management development, and employee relations outplacement."

Keep your e-mail cover letter very short. Generally it should be no more than three paragraphs or one screen in length. Use your pertinent key words, and highlight items from your resume without repeating what is there. Use standard business-letter protocol with a salutation (Dear Ms.) and complimentary close (Sincerely yours). While you can prepare the letter with any word-processing software, put it in ASCII format and place it above your e-mail resume for sending to the employer.[27]

Sending Your E-mail Resume and Letter

With your resume in an ASCII format you are now ready to distribute it. Since obtaining the e-mail address of an employer is more difficult than obtaining the physical address for a hard-copy letter and resume, your distribution should be very selective. Some job hunters obtain e-mailing lists and do a blind distribution of their resumes. Targeted distributions that are personalized with a cover letter get better results. Individuals who blindly distribute would be better-advised to post their e-resumes to a resume bank.[28]

One word of warning: Do not e-mail your resume from work. "A recent survey by the American Management Association found that 27 percent of employers monitor their employees' e-mail. Some even set up alerts when words such as *resume* appear."[29]

Resume Posting

Since the majority of companies now scan and store resumes, they have made the submission process easier by creating online resume forms. These are portions of their Web sites that are designed for you to paste your resume. As you pinpoint a

Figure 3.2 E-mail Resume

```
PAUL RIPLEY
P.O. Box 818
Oklahoma City, OK 73150
405-555-8765
pripley@aol.org


SENIOR MANAGEMENT HUMAN RESOURCES DIRECTOR POSITION

~~~~~~~~~~~~~~~
KEY-WORD SUMMARY
~~~~~~~~~~~~~~~
-Human Resources Specialist, 10 years experience in personnel
functions including management development, training, employee
relations, benefits compensation, recruitment, and outplacement.
-Certificate in ADA, Coaching, Negotiating, Myers-Briggs Type
Assessment, and TQM Training.
-Specific training skills include Computer-Based, Interactive
Video, Workplace Attitude, Diversity, Adult Learning, Needs
Analysis, Teams, Facilitation, and Group Facilitation.


~~~~~~~~~~~~~~~~~~~~~~
PROFESSIONAL EXPERIENCE
~~~~~~~~~~~~~~~~~~~~~~~~
Personnel Director, General Motors Assembly Plant,
Oklahoma City, Oklahoma, March 2000 to present.
-Report directly to Plant Manager in manufacturing facility
with 2,500 employees. Responsible for all corporate Human
Resource-related functions.
* Coordinate all recruiting, hiring, compensation management,
employee benefits packages, and pension and insurance
administration.
* Oversee labor/management/employee relations.
* Negotiated a four-year labor contract
* Reduced annual cost of Worker's Compensation Insurance and
Group Health Plan by over 25%.
* Designed and implemented policies for Family & Medical
Leave, Americans with Disabilities Act, Drug & Alcohol Abuse,
and Sexual Harassment.
~~~~~~~~~~~~~~~~~~~~~~~~~~~~~~~~~~~~~~~~~~~~~~~~~~~~~~~~~~~~
```

Figure 3.2 E-mail Resume (continued)

```
~~~~~~~~~~
PAUL RIPLEY
-2-
~~~~~~~~~~
Training Director, Dell Computers, Austin, Texas
December 1996 to February 2000.
-Reported to Vice President of Human Resources for computer
manufacturing plant of 1,500 employees.
* Designed, developed, and delivered customized training that
was determined by needs assessment.
* Coordinated all employees' training, including vendor
contracting for on-site programs.
* Reduced in-house cost of personal computer (PC) training
by 27%.
* Designed database system for recording employee-training
records as part of ISO 9000 compliance.
* Provided company's highly popular diversity training
program to 20 corporate clients.

Human Resource Generalist, Hallmark Corporation,
Kansas City, Missouri, June 1994 to November 1996.
- Reported to Human Resource Director for greeting card
company with 2,000 employees.
* Successfully recruited artists, designers, programmers,
and managers for corporate office.
* Wrote interviewing manual for supervisors and managers.
* Designed campus interview process for recruiters.

Trainer, Fred Pryor Training, Kansas City, Kansas
June 1992 to June 1994.
-Reported to owner of pre-packaged seminar company.
* Initiated start-up functions for needs analysis and
development of 25 client training programs.
* Created and developed 12 in-house training courses.
* Instructed five "public seminars" at sites across the
nation and in Canada.
* Gained overview of training field through temporary
assignments for several clients.
* Wrote copy for bi-monthly newsletter.
~~~~~~~~~~~~~~~~~~~~~~~~~~~~~~~~~~~~~~~~~~~~~~~~~~~~~~~~~~~~
```

Figure 3.2 E-mail Resume (concluded)

```
~~~~~~~~~~
PAUL RIPLEY
-3-
~~~~~~~~~~

~~~~~~~~~~
EDUCATION
~~~~~~~~~~
Executive Master of Business Administration, concentration
in Human Resources, 2003
University of Oklahoma, Norman, Oklahoma
Bachelor of Business Administration, 1994
University of Kansas, Lawrence, Kansas

Additional Professional Training
Human Resource Director Program, 2002
Harvard Business School, Boston, Massachusetts
Certificate in Human Relations, 2001
University of Oklahoma, Norman, Oklahoma


~~~~~~~~~~~~~~~~~~~~~~~~~
PROFESSIONAL ORGANIZATIONS
~~~~~~~~~~~~~~~~~~~~~~~~~
* American Society for Training & Development
* Human Resource Exchange
* Society for Human Resource Management
* Toastmaster's International
```

certain company that you would like to approach for an interview, check out whether it has an online application process incorporated into its Web site. An ASCII resume is best for this posting.

Commercial resume banks and job-search databases, discussed at the beginning of this chapter, require senders to manually input text into forms provided on their sites. Each site has separate instructions for how to cut and paste your resume to an appropriate field on the form. You may have to alter the resume each time you submit it. Remember that a cover letter is also appropriate at these sites, so always paste in your letter before you paste your resume.

A variety of job-search databases exist. Your success in getting an interview from someone who finds your resume through a database is probably enhanced in times of low unemployment and according to your field of expertise. Job databases normally fall into five groupings:

1. *National databases* that cover many nationwide occupations and industries.
2. *Geographically specific databases* that cover jobs in certain regions within the United States.
3. *Industry-specific databases* such as accounting, engineering, legal, and health care.
4. *International databases* for job positions worldwide.[30]

When using these services, online resume expert Rebecca Smith suggests, "Base your initial selection of web-based resume databases on what industry you want to work in, what your experience level is, and how confidential you want your job search to be. Follow up your selection with criteria such as overall reputation, . . . cost, and ability to update and delete your resume at will."[31]

Online Web Resume

To show employers your technological abilities, placing your resume on the web can be a smart move. Creating a web resume is especially important if you are a graphic designer, web page developer, or multimedia specialist. It allows potential employers to view your resume as a "virtual portfolio" of your work. However, making it accessible on the web is not always easy. Most job boards, such as Monster.com, explicitly prohibit HTML resumes. Unless you are a college student whose university will provide limited housing space, you will need to find a commercial Web hosting provider.

There are several advantages to Web resumes:

- You can add pictures, distinctive fonts, navigation buttons, audio and video clips, and links to created projects—although overuse of these devices can quickly destroy the resume's quality.
- You don't have to be an HTML whiz to design this resume. Numerous software packages (Adobe Page Mill, Microsoft Front Page, or Claris Home Page) allow even inexperienced designers a chance to get started.
- Employers can access your resume around the clock. Potential employers can even find you by accident while passively surfing the web.
- If you want a job in any phase of web design, putting your work on a Web site is imperative.

Remember that an HTML and a PDF resume are not the same. While the HTML resume is housed on the Internet, it can be changed. PDF documents are entered on the Internet, and have the advantage of looking the same on every machine—yet they cannot be altered. In fact, sending a PDF file to an employer to place in a company database would first require that the employer print out the document and then scan it into a database. These are steps most employers would not take unless you are a very special job applicant.

If you construct a Web resume keep a couple of things in mind: First, organize the resume smartly with a clean layout. Keep it simple so an employer's browser will be sure to access it. When you upload it onto the Internet check your download time. A good rule of thumb is that a Web page should never take longer than 28 seconds to download. If your pages take longer drop some images or make them smaller.[32]

Rebecca Smith's e-resumes and resources Web site has some excellent examples of Web resumes. Check out the following URLs to see the characteristics of this resume option.[33]

Network Administrator http://www.atomicweb.net/littleasia/resume.html

Graphic Designer, Computer Visual Communications http://www.geocities.com/Area51/Stargate/7998/jopag.html

Senior Employee Benefits Attorney http://benefitsattorney.com/resume.html

Technical Lead or Senior Analyst/Developer http://jowsey.com/resume/index.html

Notes

1. Useen, J. (1999, July 5). For sale online: You. *Fortune*, pp. 66–78; and Fisher, R. (2001, January 22). Enjoy being unemployed? Keep job hunting online. *Fortune*, p. 164.
2. Dikel, M.F. (2001). The Riley Guide: Employment Opportunities and Job Resources on the Internet. Retrieved October 13, 2002, at **http://www.dbm.com/jobguide/**
3. Pearce, C.G. & Tuten, T.L. (2001, March). Internet recruiting in the banking industry. *Business Communication Quarterly*, pp. 9–18.
4. Corsini, S. (2001, June). Wired to hire. *Training*, pp. 50–54.
5. American net users search for jobs online. (2002, July 23). Report by Pew Internet and American Life. Retrieved October 13, 2002, at **http://www.nua.ie/surveys/index.cgi?f=VS&art_id=905358199&rel=true**
6. In search of the perfect career opportunity. (1999, Summer). *Journal of Career Planning & Employment, 59*, 4, pp. 31–37.
7. Top 500 companies recruit personnel online. (2002, April 12). Report by iLogas Research. Retrieved October 13, 2002, at **http://www.nua.ie/surveys/index.cgi?f=VS&art_id=905357843&rel=true**
8. Pearch, C.G. & Tuten, T.L. pp. 9–18.
9. Useem, J. & Fisher, R.
10. Kerka, S. (2001). Job searching in the 21st century: Myths and realities. ERIC Clearinghouse on Adult, Career and Vocational Education, 14. Retrieved October 13, 2002, at **http://www.ericacve.org/docgen.asp?tbl=mr&ID=104**

11. York, T. (1999, May 3). Net matches up employers, job seekers. *Investor Business Daily*, p. A7.
12. Bolles, R. N. (2001) *Job-Hunting on the Internet*. 3rd ed. (p. 1). Berkley, CA: Ten Speed Press.
13. Dixon, P. & Tiersten, S. (1995). *Be Your Own Headhunter Online*. (pp. 4–5). New York: Random House.
14. Bolles, R. N. Job Hunters Bible.com can be found at **http://www.jobhuntersbible.com/jobs/listsites.shtml**
15. Most job seekers stay faithful to one Web site. (2002, May 7). Report from Jupiter Research. Retrieved October 13, 2002, from **http://www.nua.ie/surveys/index.cgi?f=VS&art_id=905357922&rel=true**; Monster top of job search sites ranking. (2001, June 15). Report from Greenfield Online. Retrieved October 13, 2002, at **http://www.nua.ie/surveys/index.cgi?f=VS&art_id=905356875&rel=true**; Monster leads global online recruiting market. (2001, March 22). Report from IDC Research. Retrieved October 13, 2002, at **http://www.nua.ie/surveys/index.cgi?f=VS&art_id=905356580&rel=true**
16. The net guide: Your resume. (n.d.). Job Hunters Bible.com. Retrieved October 13, 2002, at **http://www.jobhuntersbible.com/resumes/fgmresumes.shtml**
17. *Ibid*.
18. The net guide: Job listings. (n.d.). Job Hunters Bible.com. Retrieved October 13, 2002, at **http://www.jobhuntersbible.com/jobs/fgmjobs.shtml**
19. MIT Careers Handbook. (n.d.). Retrieved April 2, 2002, at **http://web.mit.edu/career/www/handbook/resumescan.html**
20. Optimize your resume as a key word resume. (n.d.) CareerPerfect.com. Retrieved October 1, 2002, at **http://www.careerperfect.com/CareerPerfect/resumes1.htm**
21. Weddle, P. D. (1995, August 6–12). Write a high-powered electronic resume. *National Business Employment Weekly*, p. 22.
22. Creating a scannable resume. (n.d.). Lincoln Laboratory, Massachusetts Institute of Technology. (p. 3). Retrieved October 17, 2002, at **http://www.ll.mit.edu/careers/pdf/ScannableResume.pdf**
23. Optimize your resume as a key word resume, p. 1.
24. *Ibid*.
25. Create a scannable version of your key word resume. (n.d.). CareerPerfect.com. Retrieved October 17, 2002, at **http://www.careerperfect.com/CareerPerfect/resumes3.htm**
26. Gilles, J. How to create and send an e-mail resume. (n.d.) ZDNet. Retrieved October 14, 2002, at **http://www.zdnet.com/products/stories/reviews/0,4161,914823,00.html**; Create an ASCII version of your key word resume. (n.d.). CareerPerfect.com. Retrieved October 18, 2002, at **http://www.careerperfect.com/CareerPerfect/resumes2.htm** ASCII resume tutorial. (n.d.). Rebecca Smith's eResumes and Resources. Retrieved September 6, 2002, at **http://www.eresume.com/tut_asciiresume.html**
27. Hansen, R. S. Tips for a dynamic e-mail cover letter. (n.d.). Quintessential Careers Web site. Retrieved September 6, 2002, at **http://www.quintcareers.com/email_cover_letters.html**
28. Sending cover letters electronically. (n.d.). Rebecca Smith's eResumes and Resources. Retrieved September 6, 2002, at **http://www.eresumes.com/tut_ecoverletters.html**
29. More U.S. firms checking e-mail, computer files, and phone calls, says American Management Association survey. (2002, April 14). American Management Association. Retrieved October 19, 2002, at **http://www.amanet.org/press/research/check_email.htm**
30. Smith, R. The FAQs of posting resumes online. (n.d.) Rebecca Smith's eResumes and Resources. Retrieved September 6, 2002, at **http://www.eresumes.com/tut_posting.html**

31. *Ibid.*
32. Parker, E. (1998, April 1). Anatomy of a killer web resume. *Computerworld.* Retrieved September 6, 2002, at **http://www.computerworld.com/news/1998/story/0,11280,30389,00.html**
33. Best of the web resumes. (n.d.). Rebecca Smith's eResumes and Resources. Retrieved September 6, 2002, at **http://www.eresumes.com/tut_webrezpicks.html**

CHAPTER - 4

Employment Correspondence

After you have assembled both your standard and electronic resumes you should consider the types of employment correspondence that you may need to write. This section addresses three primary letter types (cover, cold-call, and thank-you). Ideas are then suggested for five secondary letter types (oversubscribed interviews, acknowledging an offer, accepting an offer, declining an offer, and inquiring about the status of your application). All of these letters use the format of standard business letters and include the necessary letter parts: date, correct address, return address, signature, and enclosure statement.

Every letter is a part of your image projection; consider the purpose and impact of each one carefully. Sample letters give you an overview of how certain things fit into the letter's content. But remember that generic letters are impersonal and cold. Be sure your letters are tailored to the purpose of your job search, and to the person you desire to impress and persuade. In other words, put a lot of thought, creativity, and feeling into each letter. Create a natural, conversational tone. Be brief, concise and specific. Write like a pro, make copies of everything you write, and send the letters with confidence.

Letter Format

Employment letters should be written in paragraph form. While bulleted lists work for resumes, they lack the formal design yet conversational tone needed when writing potential employers. While the letters are about "selling you," it is important that they be employer and job-centered and not self-centered.

Generally you should use a direct approach for your content. This means stating the most important information first, followed by the next-most important, and next-most important. In certain instances where you are writing to someone you do not know, or are declining a job offer, you may want to follow the indirect approach. That approach allows you to use a buffer in the first paragraph followed by the most important information. Overall, the letters should be easy and enjoyable to read. Each paragraph should be written so that the reader wants to continue reading the next one. Write so the reader will have a smile on his or her face after reading the letter.

Employment letters should be prepared on standard 8½-by-11-inch high-quality paper. Many people prefer that the stationery for their letters match that used for their resumes. If you choose this approach try to also match the envelope to the stationery. It is best to type your envelopes and to address each envelope with the full name and title of the contact person in your letter.

Generally employment cover letters fit into three or four paragraphs. As with the resume it is good to also strive for a one-page limit for your letters. Make the margins wide enough so that the reader can jot notes while reading it.

Your letters should be clean and attractive to the eye. Proofread the letters several times. The spelling, grammar, sentence structure, and punctuation should all be perfect. Remember, every error tarnishes the positive image you seek to project, and it translates to how you will perform if hired.

Cover Letter

Most job applicants will receive a job offer as a result of an interview, not in direct response to sending or posting a resume. Yet in many job searches, situations arise in which you will not be able to talk to an employer in person. On those occasions a good cover letter may win you an important interview or a job. A cover letter is sent with a resume as a way of introducing the job applicant.

The cover letter, like a resume, is in reality a marketing tool. The primary purpose is to sell your image to an employer. Yet just like with a resume, an employer will often spend only a few seconds glancing at the letter before deciding your fate. It is critical that your letter persuade the reader.

You are "the brand" your cover letter is selling. Good marketing tools concentrate on the buyer, not the seller. Instead of presenting a "seeking" approach, your cover letter should be receiver-oriented. A statement like, "I am seeking a challenging opportunity" should be redirected to say, "You will receive a creative, productive leader with a proven track record."

Another important receiver factor is that the person who will receive, read, and decide the fate of your letter and resume must be the person who has the power to hire you. While that person is usually a stranger to you, personalizing the letter can give the impression that you are seated across the desk and ready to answer interview questions. Your letter should be brief and to the point, neat, accurate in every respect, and it should quickly move the reader to your resume.

Personalization requires that you do your homework about the job and the company. You should research every company and industry that you plan to contact by letter. In the body of your letter allow your reader to see the result of that research, and how your skills will truly meet the company's needs. Four key topics should be included in the cover letter. These items generally constitute complete paragraphs. Figure 4.1 lists them in the preferred order.

Never use a salutation like "Dear Madam," "Dear Sir," or "To Whom It May Concern." This is a direct admission to the reader that you did not do your homework. Instead, address your letter to a specific person. If you do not know the specific person to send it to, call the company—regardless of where it might be—and obtain the name of the correct source, the proper spelling of that person's name, the person's title, and the company address. Discovering the right person, and personalizing a letter to that individual, nonverbally communicates an added level of effort and immediately presents a professional image of you.

A good cover letter should always describe the specific position for which you are applying and the skills and qualities that you can offer an employer. Chapter 1

Figure 4.1 Content of an Application Letter

                                                     Your full address with Zip code
                                                     Date

Employer's name
Title
Company name
Full address with Zip code

Dear_____:

(Paragraph 1) This paragraph tells who you are and why you are writing. Identify the specific position you are applying for, explain how you learned of it, and state your desire to be an applicant.

(Paragraph 2) Describe your understanding of the job requirements, why you are interested in the company or field of work, and what you have to offer.

(Paragraph 3) In this paragraph describe how you specifically meet, and even exceed, the requirements of the job. Refer the reader to your resume and skills. Briefly describe your main qualifications (education and work experience). Stress your strongest offerings that relate to the job or field.

(Paragraph 4) Request an interview or an answer to your letter. Display positive eagerness here. While you should give your phone number, with area code, you will find it more advantageous to call the employer after a few days. Thank the person for the time spent reading the material, and for considering your application.

                                                    Complimentary closing
                                                    (Sincerely or Truly Yours,)

                                                    (Your handwritten signature)

                                                    Your full name (typed)

Enclosure (your resume)

described many of those characteristics and listed five that are considered by employers to be most important: (1) Communication skills (both oral and written); (2) Teamwork and interpersonal skills; (3) Leadership skills; (4) Professional and technical proficiency; and (5) Self-management skills (drive, self-motivation, ambition, integrity, and initiative).

Other sought-after skills and characteristics are also critical to use. They include:

- Organizational skills
- Entrepreneurial skills
- Self-confidence
- Problem-solving skills
- Flexibility
- Ability to sell ideas and persuade others
- Ability to acquire technical, analytical, and foreign-language skills quickly
- Ability to follow orders[1]

In your cover letter describe how your previous training and experience have equipped you with any of those skills. Table 4.1 gives a list of several self-descriptive words that can be used in highlighting your skills. Figure 4.2 displays a sample cover letter that uses some of these self-descriptive words.

Table 4.1 Self-Descriptive Words for Employment Letters

Active	Economical	Perceptive
Adaptable	Efficient	Personable
Aggressive	Energetic	Pleasant
Alert	Enterprising	Positive
Ambitious	Enthusiastic	Practical
Analytical	Extroverted	Productive
Attentive	Fair	Realistic
Broad-minded	Forceful	Resourceful
Conscientious	Imaginative	Respective
Constructive	Independent	Self-Reliant
Creative	Logical	Sense of Humor
Dependable	Loyal	Sincere
Determined	Mature	Sophisticated
Diplomatic	Methodical	Systematic
Disciplined	Objective	Tactful
Discrete	Optimistic	Talented

Source: Adapted from Powell, C.R. *Career Planning Today*, 2nd edition. (p. 136). Dubuque, IA: Kendall-Hunt.

Figure 4.2 Sample Cover Letter

2433 Cox Street
Chicago, IL 73549
February 5, 2003

Mr. Stephen Watts
Vice-President of Training
Macy's Department Store
2500 Park Avenue
New York, NY 20062

Dear Mr. Watts:

I am excited that Macy's Department Store has recently opened a new store in the Chicago suburb. I am interested in joining your energetic team as a member of the buyer training program.

Macy's stands for quality in the Chicago area. I have long had a desire to be a part of your quality organization and to use my communication and team skills in your buyers program. Macy's method of having buyers serve as department managers is especially attractive since I have actively managed several work groups.

In May 2003, I will graduate from the University of Chicago with a Masters of Business Administration with a concentration in marketing. Throughout my academic program, I have taken courses to complement my business degree. Specific courses that I believe have helped prepare me for a career in retailing are advanced psychology, fashion design, layout, organizational behavior, management, interpersonal communications, accounting, and computer science. As you will note on my enclosed resume, I have supplemented my formal course work with cooperative education work experience at Nordstrom's Department Store. I believe that this work experience, coupled with my academic background, makes me an excellent choice for your buyer training program.

May I meet and talk with you, at your earliest convenience, regarding my interest in Macy's? I will call your office in a few days for an appointment.

Sincerely,

Stephanie Moore-Jones

Stephanie Moore-Jones

Enclosure: Resume

Cold-Call Letter

In their eagerness to find work, some applicants gather numerous names of organizations and send out unsolicited targeted resumes en masse. While this approach is designed to tap hidden job markets, the likelihood of receiving an interview is low. Nevertheless, because many try this approach, Figure 4.3 gives some hints for what can be included in a cold-call letter.

If you decide to use this approach, make your letter brief, and do not restate information contained in your resume. Be sure to address the letter to a specific person; otherwise it will be sent to the personnel department, which is an immediate dead end. It is also vital that you personalize your message to avoid the look of a form letter.

Since you will probably be unsure of specific job positions available with the company, your letter should take a different slant. Focus on broader occupational possibilities and elements that show that you are familiar with the organization and that you know how your qualifications would fit the company.

If you are responding to an ad in a newspaper regarding a specific position, analyze the job description in the ad carefully for key words that can be used to identify the key skills the employer is seeking. In your letter use those same key words to create key-word paragraph headings.

Thank-You Letter

Immediately following an information or job interview with a company you should rush home and prepare a thank-you letter to the key people you talked with. Mail it the same day, if possible. Interviewers are mixed on whether the thank-you should be formal (typed) or informal (hand written). The culture of the organization will give you a good indication. If in doubt, type it.

The thank-you letter should be warm, personally focused, and professional in tone. Send it even though you probably said your thanks at the end of the interview. Never fax a thank-you letter. Type it instead on heavy vellum stationery, and never use an employer's letterhead. Tradition also tends toward not e-mailing your thank-you. This is especially true if the interviewer is a traditionalist, or if you don't want a copy of the e-mail placed in your file. However, a recent survey by Accountemps of 150 executives with the nation's 1,000 largest companies found that 78 percent felt it is now appropriate to e-mail a thank-you note.[2] You should use e-mail if quick action matters, if that was the way you sent your resume, if you are dealing with a high-tech firm, and if your instinct tells you it is the right conduct.[3]

While you may never hear from the company, a thank-you letter indicates your maturity and understanding of good business etiquette. Such responses will impress the right person. An initial thank-you letter should express your appreciation for the employer's time and reaffirm your interest in the position and company. It also is where you can clarify things discussed in the interview, and even add information you did not have a chance to mention.[4] If an additional interview materializes, your next thank-you letter could also mention your gratitude in relation to any of the following situations that apply:

1. The company paid your out-of-town transportation charges and hotel expenses.
2. You met with future colleagues and discussed the job and the company.

Figure 4.3 Content of a Cold-Call Targeted Letter

> Your full address and Zip code
> Date
>
> Name of person
> Person's title
> Company name
> Company address with Zip code
>
> Dear_____:
>
> (Paragraph 1) State your desire, as an upcoming graduate, to work for this company. Mention any training programs or work areas for which you would like to be considered.
>
> (Paragraph 2) Refer the reader to your resume and briefly highlight the areas that relate to the company's field.
>
> (Paragraph 3) Request an interview or consideration for the job.
>
> Complimentary closing
>
> (Your handwritten signature)
>
> Your full name (typed)
>
> Enclosure (your resume)

3. You were allowed to observe the work in a department where you will be working, or you were able to observe the work in several departments through which you would rotate during a training program.
4. You were shown various parts of the city, including potential areas where you might want to live.
5. You were offered the job and now:
   - Wish to consider it,
   - Wish to discuss it with your partner, or
   - Wish to accept or reject it.
6. If no offer was made, but you want to remain an applicant, express continued interest and a desire to either furnish additional information or participate in additional interviews.

A sample thank-you letter is found in Figure 4.4.

Figure 4.4 Sample Thank-You Letter

6115 Dolby Avenue
Colorado Springs, CO 94321
March 13, 2003

Ms. Sharla Barber, President
Barber/Fox Advertising Agency
P.O. Box 1452
Colorado Springs, CO 94325

Dear Ms. Barber:

Thank you for your time and courtesy in meeting with me on Monday regarding your position for an account executive at Barber/Fox. The tour of your advertising facility and the conversations with your staff gave me a clear picture of the accounts that I would be supervising. I was especially impressed with your creative talent and your newly computerized accounting process.

My visit to the Barber/Fox Agency has reaffirmed my desire to be a part of your organization. The excitement, high energy level, and fast pace are exactly what I like. I believe my previous account experience with The Richards Group in Dallas, and my sales work with Dell Computer in Austin, Texas, qualify me for your position.

If there are additional items you would like for me to send please let me know. I would welcome the opportunity to work for Barber/Fox. I look forward to hearing from you soon.

Sincerely,

Ann Foley

Ann Foley

Additional Employment Letters

A variety of additional employment letters often need to be written. Use the following general descriptions to organize those letters if the occasion arises.

Oversubscribed Placement Center Interviews

When you have been unable to secure an interview with a company through your campus career center, it is proper to send the interviewer a letter requesting an interview. The following items should be addressed in the letter:

1. State your attempt to interview on campus, yet your inability to secure a slot on the sign-up sheet.
2. Ask for an interview at the employer's convenience.
3. State your willingness to cover any expenses involved.
4. Refer the employer to your enclosed resume.

Acknowledging an Offer

Whenever you receive an offer from a company you should always request a letter confirming the offer and the specifics of it. Upon receiving the offer you should also acknowledge immediately that offer with a personal letter. The following elements will need to be addressed:

1. Acknowledge the company's offer.
2. Express thanks and your happiness for having received the offer.
3. If you are considering the offer, or need time to make a decision because of possible offers from other companies, state your need for time to make a decision and the date by which you will notify the company of your decision.

If you have decided to accept the offer your letter needs to follow a different format.

Accepting an Offer

In the opening paragraph you accept the offer and refer to the date of the letter or telephone call whereby the offer was made. Also state your excitement about becoming an employee of the company. A sample letter of an offer of acceptance is found in Figure 4.5.

The second paragraph is more detailed. Here you have an opportunity to state your understanding of the specific conditions of employment. Remember however, that this letter is not the tool to use in negotiating salary conditions or benefits. Those items should be hashed out face-to-face or on the telephone, and preferably before you write this letter. The acceptance letter is your confirmation that you agree to what has been resolved. Some of the things you may be agreeing to are: salary, bonus, starting date, office location, expense policies, travel schedules, and benefits. This second paragraph is where you should state that information.

Finally, the closing paragraph is the location for restating your warm appreciation of the offer, and your pleasure in becoming a member of the team. It is also an appropriate place to describe your plans and how you can be contacted between the letter's date and your starting date.

Declining an Offer

If you decline a job offer it is common courtesy to acknowledge that decline with a letter. While you are saying "no" in the letter, use the opportunity to create a positive parting impression with the reader. Some people who decline a job offer find that either they or the company will recontact at a later date.

Figure 4.5 Sample Acceptance Letter

> P.O. Box SMU 152
> Dallas, TX 75555
> May 10, 2003
>
> Mr. Gene Burns
> Training Director
> West-Tex Corporation
> 1200 W. Commerce
> Dallas, TX 75205
>
> Dear Mr. Burns:
>
> I was excited to open my mail today and see your letter, offering me a position in the training program at West-Tex. I accept! As I told you during our interview and in my correspondence, West-Tex has been the organization I have dreamed of working for.
>
> As we agreed the starting salary will be $50,000, and I will receive a total monthly expense account of $500. This will include general expenses for cellular phone, meals, and auto expenses. A car from the car pool will be assigned to me during the first year. After that time we will negotiate my auto allowance.
>
> The starting date of July 5, 2003, will work perfectly. I am sure we will talk several times prior to my arrival on that date, so any information that you need from me I will be happy to furnish.
>
> I look forward to seeing you, and joining my colleagues in the training program at West-Tex on July 5.
>
> Sincerely,
>
> *Herb Finch*
>
> Herb Finch

In the first paragraph thank the employer for the offer and the opportunity to interview with the company employees. In paragraph two decline the offer and give your reason. Let the employer know that you considered the opportunity carefully. Word your response in such a way that the reader retains a very positive impression of you. Finally, express your appreciation for the company's interest in you and for a pleasant interview experience. Figure 4.6 displays a sample letter that declines a job offer.

Employment letters are a required part of the job-search process. While there are general formats for the different kinds of letters that you may be required to write, it is important that each letter be written in a professional way. Every job

Figure 4.6 Sample Letter Declining an Offer

> 12 Lions Way
> Memphis, TN 30301
> May 10, 2003
>
> Mr. George Clark, President
> First America Bank
> P.O. Box 1421
> St. Paul, MN 80522
>
> Dear Mr. Clark:
>
> Thank you for your letter of May 7, 2003, offering me the position of financial analyst with First America Bank.
>
> I must decline your offer because I accepted a position last week with First Republic Bank in Nashville.
>
> While I was waiting for the last six weeks to hear from you, I was contracted by the people at First Republic. While the job and salary are comparable, the First Republic position allows me to stay in Tennessee and be closer to my aging parents.
>
> The decision not to accept your offer was difficult. I enjoyed so much the interest you showed in me and the wonderful climate displayed by the employees at First America. While I will not be working with you, I will long remember the positive impression that you made. I wish you and your staff at First America the best.
>
> Sincerely,
>
> *Mary Lewis-Ryan*
>
> Mary Lewis-Ryan

applicant has a resume. Most job applicants write some form of employment letter. Most of these letters cover the basic information that needs to be stated. The best letters are thoughtful, personal, creative, and upbeat. They stand out. Take the time to make your letters totally professional.

Notes

1. Emphasizing your transferable and marketable skills in your cover letter. (n.d.). Quintessential Careers Web site. Retrieved September 6, 2002, at **http://www.quintcareers.com/cover_letter_transferable_skills.html**

2. Interview etiquette. (2002, October 9). *USA Today*, 1A.
3. Useem, J. (1999, July 5). For sale online: You. *Fortune*, 67–78.
4. Cover letters and business correspondence. (n.d.). Publication of The Weston Career Resources Center, Olin School of Business, Washington University in St. Louis. Retrieved October 4, 2002, at **http://olin.wustl.edu/wcrc/sstudents/ugrad/letters.cfm**

CHAPTER - 5

The Job Interview

Chapters 2 and 3 presented the need for a thoroughly developed, well-written resume. Chapter 4 described the formulas for several employment-related letters. While resumes and employment letters are crucial, they are marketing tools and their primary objective is to help you obtain a job interview.

The **job interview** is important for both the company and you. In it your potential employer measures the value of your talents against the needs of the company and tries to determine whether you would be satisfied with the position and would be willing to make a true commitment to the organization. The interview is your best opportunity to sell yourself to your prospective employer. You should leave the interview with a better understanding of the company, whether or not there is good chemistry between you and the company, and whether or not you truly want the job. If there is a match you need to convince the employer that you are qualified for the position and that you will be a positive asset to the company.

Interviewers approach interviews with those currently employed differently than they do with students. If you are currently employed an interviewer will probably assume your work experience has given you some job maturity. They also assume that you have given more thought to your career and have spent considerable time researching the company. Since being currently employed places you in a higher pay range, interviewers will expect more from their interviews with you.

If you are an advanced business student the assumption may be that your continued focus on education and your possible internship and work experience give you a desire to start and learn a profession. This chapter will give you an understanding of what to expect during interviews and how to prepare for them. It starts by first describing some ways you can learn information about the company. It then reviews different types of interviews and questioning approaches. Third, methods of preparation are discussed. The chapter will conclude with tips on how to successfully make the interview count.

Preparing for the Interview

Once you secure an interview there are several preparatory steps to consider.

Prepare Yourself

You have conducted your career planning, you have created your resume, now prepare yourself mentally to discuss the "real you" with an interviewer. In your preparation review the list of transferable skills that you developed in Chapter 1. What are your key accomplishments in life? How would you describe your management style? What are your personal and professional strengths? As you consider these areas "script" out possible answers to the questions. You will find this to be of considerable help when you start preparing answers to possible interview questions that can be asked.[1]

Understand the Company

Do Your Homework about the Company

According to a Chicago magazine marketing director many university graduates today are woefully unprepared for interviews. When she was recently hiring a marketing assistant for her magazine, she found the following: "Only two of the dozen candidates I met with bothered to locate a copy of our magazine in advance. . . . One young man . . . arrived completely unprepared, sans notebook, pen, or pencil. Several other candidates asked, 'What's the magazine about and who reads it?' Another [asked], 'Do you really think there's a future in the marketing track?'[2] David Elyer, author of *Job Interviews That Mean Business*, confirmed interviewees' lack of preparedness. He found that less than 20 percent of the candidates that he had interviewed over the years had done any preliminary research on the company where they interviewed.[3]

As you approach the interview process it is important that you learn as much as possible about the organization that you will interview with. Reading the annual report is only a start. Read articles in *Fortune, Business Week,* and *The Wall Street Journal* that will allow you to talk about the company's strengths and weaknesses. In particular, research the following aspects of the organization.[4]

The Organization's Industry

- Is the organization in a stable or a cyclical industry?
- What is the current and potential growth of the industry?
- What is the future outlook for the industry?

The Company

- Is the company public or privately held?
- What is the dollar volume of the organization's annual business?
- How many employees work for the organization?
- What products or services does the organization manufacture or provide?
- Are the products or services diversified?
- Is the scope of the organization international, national, or regional?
- What is the overall growth potential of the organization?
- What is the history of the organization's culture?
- Is the organization stable?
- Is there a threat of merger or possible buyout by others?
- What are the names of the top executives in the organization?

- How would you describe the organization's management?
- What are the personnel policies that can affect you?
- What are the organization's social and economic goals?
- Has the organization had any ethical violations?
- What are the general contents of the annual report?

You can learn such details through your campus library, by talking to personal contacts and alumni, by reading company literature, and through an Internet search.

One of the best resources is to study the company's Web site. As you examine the Web site ask yourself the following questions. Is the layout traditional or creatively high-tech? Is the language used formal or casual? Are pictures of top management formal or relaxed? What kinds of stories can you find about the company? Are there profiles of management, stories of the company culture, or a company newsgroup? As you read about the company make a note of adjectives used to describe the company's leadership and employees. Look at your own list of transferable skills. Which of your skills matches those used by the company?[5]

The Company's Values While knowing about the company's industry, products, and economic success, it is also critical to determine if your personal core values are the same as those espoused by the company. As Chapter 1 described, information of this type is found in the company's mission and value statements, and its code of ethics. Organizations want to make sure that your core values equate to theirs. Savio Chan, president and CEO of Technology Training Solutions, contends that most people regard technical competence as the number-one requirement of potential new hires. "I beg to differ . . . technical competence is number two when hiring; the most important thing to look for is if the interviewee understands where the company is going and agrees with its core values."[6]

According to Taunee Besson, president of Dallas, Texas–based Career Dimensions, answers to the following questions will tell you about an employer's environment before you accept an offer.

- Does the employer have clear goals and live by them?
- Is the employer's strategic plan understood and embraced by all levels?
- How effective are the company's communications?
- Are employees a part of a team?
- Is the company open to change?
- Do employees have fun?
- Do individual employees have the chance to make contributions?
- What training is available?
- How does the firm reward employees?
- Does the company have a development plan for each employee?
- Do employees share in company profits?
- What is the firm's customer focus?[7]

With these preliminary items researched, you can often decide whether or not the company and its job is a good "fit" for you. If there is information you have been unable to find, make note of it so you can ask the employer about it during the interview.

According to Austin, having a good understanding of the company is critical for a successful interview. She lists seven things that when done, make a good impression on the interviewer:

1. Research my organization.
2. Prepare good questions for me.
3. Tell me what you can do for me, not how the job might further your personal growth.
4. Be tenacious.
5. Follow up.
6. Beware of shortcuts.
7. Remember the golden rule.[8]

Types of Interviews

There are several types of employment interviews. Consider the type that you will be participating in and follow the appropriate preparation guidelines below.

Screening Interview

The purpose of the screening interview is to conduct a "first-cut" brief evaluation of a candidate. Typically it is conducted in a college or university placement center. Usually someone other than the person you would be working for conducts the interview. While a company's personnel department employees often screen undergraduates, a division manager or someone with ties to the university, such as an alumnus, usually screens MBA candidates. The typical breakdown for a thirty-minute screening interview is:

Interviewer's objectives	2 minutes
You talk	10–15 minutes
Interviewer gives you company data	5 minutes
You can ask questions—interviewer answers	5 minutes
Interviewer tells how the decision will be made	2 minutes
Interviewer concludes the interview	1 minute
Total time	25–30 minutes

Your objectives in the screening interview are to make a good impression and to allow sufficient information to be passed between you and the interviewer to determine whether a compatible relationship exists. If you succeed, the interviewer may plan a second interview where you can meet appropriate members of the management team and participate in a more detailed analysis of your suitability for the job.

Follow-up Interview

If the first impression was good you will typically receive a letter inviting you to a second interview at the employer's facilities. The invitation means the company desires to further investigate your qualifications, abilities, and potential. The follow-up interview will cover more in-depth topics. You can expect to meet and talk with key executives and potential peers at this meeting.

Listen carefully to all the questions in a follow-up interview. Learn to quickly compare what you see and hear to what you already know about the organization. Ask well-thought-out questions (more guidance on asking questions appears below). Be polite, friendly, and try to look relaxed.

While your overriding objectives in the screening interview are to make a good impression and survive the cut, your objectives in the second interview are to become extremely familiar with the company and to answer all questions effectively.

Social Interview

The social interview often occurs for advanced undergraduates and M.B.A.s prior to or in place of the screening interview. The event is generally a cocktail reception or dinner and is held on neutral territory (such as a downtown club) or at the company's facility. If the reception is unstructured it may not feel like an interview. You probably will be encouraged to talk about yourself and pose any questions to company representatives. Be careful! You may not know which of several people are important and are the ones to impress. The important people may be the quiet ones who are listening to your questions and answers. The best rules are to drink little, circulate a lot, remain calm, ask well-thought-out questions, and respond with confidence but not cockiness.

Behavioral Interview

Your personality and a few good answers can get you through the screening interview and maybe even the second interview. But when you undergo a behavioral interview you cannot bluff your way through the answers. "Behavioral interviews are the in thing for human resource experts and personnel consultants from coast to coast who now stress finding out what a person is going to do on the job, not just verifying that he or she has the credentials to do it."[9] Some consider the behavioral interview to be the best predictor of future behavior, since past behavior is analyzed so carefully.

Organizations that use the behavioral-interview approach first develop clear job descriptions. They then identify and prioritize the quality dimensions necessary for achieving success in the position (such as planning, problem solving, decision making, selling, leadership, or organizational skills). Finally, they design open-ended questions that will allow each interviewer to determine if an applicant possesses the dimensions.

While behavioral interviews are tough, they are also fair. Since the questions are based on specific job requirements, illegal and irrelevant issues are avoided. Further, every applicant for a specific job is asked the same set of questions. The detailed job description is not offered until the interview is over, and interviewers ". . . are trained to avoid reacting to your replies or asking leading questions that betray their preferences."[10]

Behavioral interviewers go beyond the general questions about your job performance and training. Instead they center on *how* and *what* you did in very concrete terms. In the selection interview you may score points by telling the interviewer about a team project that you worked on. In the behavioral interview the interviewer will ask questions to determine whether the information is accurate or misleading. Did you help or hinder the team? To what extent did you contribute? Did the team meet the original objectives? Was the project finished on time, under or over budget? According to Eyler, "Each problem is designed to draw you out and make you demonstrate your ability to deal with problems, show your strengths and weaknesses, and help interviewers judge whether you have the skills and personal characteristics that will make you a successful part of the organization."[11]

To arrive at accurate answers skilled behavioral interviewers use the **STAR** method. This stands for:

The *S*ituation or *T*ask that the candidate experienced;
The *A*ction taken by the candidate; and
The *R*esult of the action.[12]

Here is one example of how a behavioral question was handled by an applicant who was told, "Give me an example of a job-related situation where you felt you were in over your head. What made you feel that way? What did you do to handle the situation?" Your response might be:

Situation or Task "The first job that I had after college was to work with my boss in producing an annual conference for over 1,000 attendees. I was highly excited about the opportunity and plans were running smoothly. But after three weeks on the job my boss took sick and was out of the office for over four weeks. He returned one week before the event."

Action "I kept in constant touch by phone and e-mail. Still, I had to make major decisions in his absence, and often felt very uncomfortable in doing so. I made four trips to the conference site, which was in Chicago. I learned to bargain with the property management, figured out how to create backup plans in case speakers and vendors fell through, and even handled a minor crisis regarding meals for an off-site event."

Result "The result was a highly successful meeting. The final attendance was 100 participants more than anticipated. I found them lodging and worked out all the logistics. I brought the conference in under budget. The evaluations were the highest of any conference to date. My colleagues were highly complementary. My boss wrote a wonderful letter of praise for my file. I even received a $4,000 raise at my six-month evaluation."

Since behavioral interviews often last two hours or more it becomes difficult to remain specific on your answers. To be successful stay focused, concentrate, and avoid vague, canned, or hypothetical answers. Remember to practice the STAR method and answer each question seriously, constructively, and specifically.[13]

Assignment Interview

Assignment interviews serve as job-related test situations. Here the interviewer really wants to see how you would perform in simulated job events. You might be asked to prepare and deliver a sales presentation, analyze a financial problem, recommend a solution to a problem, or facilitate a mock meeting. "One applicant for a systems analyst post was handed a calendar, a box full of memos and messages, and a list of scheduled meetings and projects. He was then given 45 minutes to prepare a schedule and priority list."[14]

The best way to perform well on assignment interviews is to take your time, do your best, and work on being cooperative with all the other participants who might also be interviewing.

Case Interview

Closely akin to the assignment interview is the case interview. If you want a job or internship with a consulting firm you will have to master the case interview. While different firms and different interviewers use different approaches, this form of interview has become in just a few short years the most effective tool that consulting firms use to select new talent. Among the companies that regularly conduct case interviews are:

- Accenture
- Bain & Company
- Booze Allen & Hamilton
- Boston Consulting Group
- Deloitte Consulting
- McKinsey & Company
- Price Waterhouse Coopers
- Towers Perrin

The case interview consists of a worded problem, which is usually based on a real-life consulting situation that the interviewer or firm has experienced. Interviewers use it to let you get a feel for the types of problem issues that consultants work on, and to also observe how you think through and solve a real business problem on the spot. It also allows an employer to assess skill areas like: leadership, analytical ability, verbal communication, organization, quantitative ability, and flexibility. This approach has become for many candidates the most-feared and difficult form of interviewing. To master it requires specific preparation, quick thinking, and keen insight and intelligence.

The case interview usually occurs during both the screening interview and all subsequent interviews. Many job seekers find they may participate in as many as a dozen case interviews during their initial and follow-up interviews with a firm. The time allotment is usually two back-to-back half-hour sessions. In the first 30 minutes, half the time is spent discussing your background and resume. The other half is devoted to a minicase. In the last 30 minutes the major consulting case is presented for 20 minutes, with the remaining time spent in general discussion and processing.

Typical Case Categories

Brain teasers are logical questions designed to get you out of your comfort zone and thinking "outside the box." They measure creativity and problem-solving skills. Examples might be, "Why is a manhole cover round?" "How many red cars are in the United States?" Top-quality firms like Bain and McKinsey tend to not use questions of this type.

Market-sizing questions test both knowledge and the quantitative thought process. They take the form of "Guess the number . . ." and interviewers want you to use a numerical response to arrive at potential solutions. Examples might be, "How many soft drinks were consumed in the United States last year?" "What is the size of the surfboard market in the United States?" "How many gas stations are there in Dallas?" or "How much paint does it take to paint the American Airlines fleet of planes?"

Functional cases use a specific scenario and ask candidates to discuss issues like pricing, manufacturing, or profits. For example: "A well-known gourmet coffee shop chain is considering expansion into the San Francisco area. They have been successful in the Northwest; what factors should they consider?" Or "An electronics manufacturer finds that its revenues are at an all-time high, but the company is still operating at a loss. Why?"

Strategy cases focus on long-term corporate issues and invite an interviewee to speculate on issues like, "What do you think the cost of cross-country bicycles will be in five years?" or "Our client, an exclusive English automobile maker is interested in introducing an SUV into the U.S. market. Should it proceed?"

As you read these examples you might think, There is no way that I would have the answer to those questions. You would be right. In fact, the interviewer could not care less about the answer. There is never *one* right answer in a case interview. The solution is often meaningless. The interviewer wants to see how you think, reason, and communicate using a problem-solving process. Table 5.1 describes the three levels of skills that all firms look for.

As you use your different skills the interviewer will want to see your thinking and reasoning process. It is important that you display that process through an interactive mode with the interviewer. Ask questions, listen, make assumptions, and draw on models from competitive strategy, finance, marketing, operations, and management. Use the models, but don't reference them. Most case interviews should proceed through four distinct parts:

1. **Asking, Identifying, and Confirming the Information**
   - Listen carefully and absorb all the information provided;
   - Make sure you completely understand the problem;
   - Backtrack after the interviewer describes the problem and paraphrase it back to the interviewer; and
   - Clarify anything you don't understand by asking the interviewer questions, but work on making the process a conversation and not a Q&A session.
2. **Structuring Your Analysis**
   - Choose a problem-solving approach and describe it to the interviewer;
   - Break the problem into separate pieces;
   - Clearly state your hypotheses;
   - Discuss the issues one at a time;

Table 5.1 Skills Interviewers Are Looking For

Diagnostic Skills
- How sharp is your business insight?
- Do you have intellectual curiosity?
- How well do you narrow down and think about a problem?
- Do you ask good, pertinent, and practical questions?
- Do you think creatively?
- Are you inquisitive?
- Can you identify and extract the most important issue from a problem?
- How do you respond to lack of information in problem solving?
- Can you easily recognize which types of analysis are appropriate for each specific case?

Analytical Skills
- Can you follow a logical line of reasoning?
- How well do you organize and structure your answers?
- Are you good at making quick calculations while under pressure?
- Do you easily separate important facts from irrelevant facts?
- Do you find it easy to make assumptions, and are those assumptions reasonable?

Communication Skills
- Do you express yourself clearly?
- Are you a good listener?
- Do you ask good questions?
- Do you take rejection of your ideas well?
- How do you adapt to different types of information that you receive?
- How well do you defend your ideas?
- Do you present a consulting presence?
- Do you possess abundant self-confidence?
- Would you be happy as a consultant?
- Do you have the aptitude for consulting?

- Explain the logic behind your responses so the interviewer can understand your thought process;
- Address all the important issues, not just the ones you feel most comfortable with;
- Don't worry about having to constantly talk. Silence is OK!
- Use frameworks only if appropriate, such as:
  - *Porter's 5 Forces:* Barriers to Entry, Bargaining Power of Buyers, Bargaining Power of Suppliers, Availability of Substitute Products, and Level of Competition Among Firms;
  - *3C's:* Cost, Customers, Competitors;
  - *4P's:* Product, Price, Place, Promotion;

- *SWOT Analysis:* Strengths, Weaknesses, Opportunities, Threats; and
- *Profit = Revenue − Costs.*
- Use graphs, diagrams, and flowcharts to explain your thoughts.
3. **Analyzing the Problem**
   - Prioritize the issues;
   - Continue to ask relevant questions;
   - Work through your analysis out loud so the interviewer can follow your logic;
   - Always explain your reasoning when you make assumptions;
   - Continue to test your hypotheses; and
   - Study the interviewer closely for hints that can guide you in your analysis.
4. **Making a Decision and Sharing Your Recommendations**
   - Develop a solution with recommendations;
   - Summarize your analysis;
   - Add real persuasion to your conclusion; and
   - Synthesize your findings into recommendations and relate those back to the problem statement.[15]

While the case-interview process may look terrifying, consulting firms really work to make the process fun. A statement from Bain & Company states this well: "A good case interview should be an enjoyable and thoughtful discussion of business issues and problem-solving techniques. We are not looking for a 'right answer' or asking you to spit back memorized business terms, current events, or well-known frameworks. Rather, we hope to see a good dose of problem-solving skills, creativity, and common sense. A good interview will be fun and full of energy!"[16]

McKinsey & Company also attempts to make the case interview enjoyable. On its Internet Web site, McKinsey lists several common mistakes that have been made by previous interviewees. They include:

- Misunderstanding the question or answering the wrong question.
- Proceeding haphazardly through the analysis by not identifying the major issues or jumping from one to another.
- Asking too many questions without telling the interviewer why you need the information.
- Force-fitting familiar frameworks to every case even if it is an irrelevant framework.[17]

A wise interviewee will practice for the case interview. While you and your colleagues can take cases out of textbooks or create business issues that you can debate in mock interviews, the following Web sites offer sample case-interview analyses that will give you a mental head start.

McKinsey & Company offers an online interactive case about a client's need to double the number of recruits while maintaining quality and not increasing spending. The case walks you through eight different questions that you must answer before you can read the interviewer's response. It is an excellent way for someone with no experience to start the case process.

McKinsey also has two European cases that give you an international flavor. Both examples structure the problem, allow you to make recommendations and supply answers, and then show you a long list of questions that an interviewer really would ask. **http://www.mckinsey.com/careers/apply/online_casestudy/** and **http://careers.mckinsey.com/app004/case2.nsf/keyview/case_01**

The Boston Consulting Group (BCG) presents a case about a Canadian retailer with 500 stores. That retailer learns that a large U.S. retailer has just bought out the Canadian firm's competition and plans to redesign the stores using the U.S. retail concept. The question raised is, "What should the Canadian firm do?" The online case interview takes a reader through several pages of dialogue between the interviewer and interviewee. **http://www.bcg.com/careers/interview_prep/case_interview.asp**

Bain & Company has four different case situations. Each is an interactive case that allows you to develop an approach, estimate the relevant facts, synthesize your conclusions, and make a recommendation. The first case asks you to determine whether a private-equity client should invest in an Internet startup called iHardware.com. Case two involves an Australian bank that wants to understand the profitability of individual segments of its retail customer base. The third is a cookie maker that has experienced a decline in profits due to turmoil in its organizational and operational areas. The fourth case evaluates whether a private-equity fund should invest in a Singapore-based bulk container firm. All are excellent in allowing you to think, act, change your mind, revise your answers, and see the final Bain consultant's solutions. **http:205.134.84.25/bainweb/join/interview/practice_overview.asp**

Vault Consulting After you read a few of the case interview samples you may realize that candidates who make it past the second and third case interviews with the likes of Bain, McKinsey, and BCG have participated in challenging practice sessions. If you cannot figure out how to create practice case interviews, a good option is offered by Vault Consulting. The process is costly, but for a few hundred dollars you can participate in an hour case interview with professional consultants. The first 30 minutes is the actual interview. During the last 30 minutes you receive instant feedback and answers to questions. You will also be sent a detailed written evaluation. Check out the details at **http://www.vault.com/static/newsletters/html/7_8207.html**.

The Videoconferencing Interview

A few firms are making use of technology in the interviewing stage. Heidrick & Struggles, one of the nation's leading CEO headhunters, uses videoconferencing to interview potential candidates. For the firm the advantages are reduced travel and accommodation costs and the ability to interview a wider range of recruits. But, videoconference interviews are often difficult on the recruit. Many are uncomfortable with the technology and have trouble smiling, making eye contact, and in using the new process to their advantage. Added to this is the necessity to travel to a site that is equipped with videoconferencing equipment.[18] While some in the business world see an advantage in using this technology to hire at lower levels of the organization, others believe the practice can be offensive, demeaning, and an impersonal approach to recruiting a company's senior officials.[19]

As technology advances Internet job interviews will be the next step. View-Cast.com, a Dallas, Texas–based firm, has software available that will allow almost anyone with a computer to interview for that job in the comfort of home.[20]

Types of Questioning Approaches

Open Questions

Open questions are broad and unstructured and allow you to develop the answers you want the interviewer to receive. If you have prepared answers to a variety of questions you have a much broader range of possible responses. Usually these questions will have a leadoff such as, "Tell me about . . ." or "What do you think about. . . ?"

If interviewers are effective at using the open approach, you will find them listening with interest and courtesy. They use silence to reflect on or clarify what you are saying and ask "why" and "how" questions to encourage you to elaborate on certain points. Effective interviewers also avoid comments that reflect their personal values, criticism, or approval.

Yes-No Questions

Yes-no questions allow you little flexibility in your answers. Questions that check on specific dates, degrees, or schools attended might call for a yes-or-no response. The interviewer who continues to use this type of questioning is inexperienced, however. You should use the opportunity to expand your answers and even try posing questions to the interviewer.

Direct Questions

Expect direct questions like "Tell me about your major area of study" or "What were your specific job tasks when you were employed at the XYZ Company?" These questions usually relate to work/education/skills that you possess, or specific experiences that you have had in the past. This type of question calls for simple, clearly thought-out, and intelligent answers. In answering these questions, as in all others, avoid contradicting yourself and answer each question truthfully.

While you should supply answers to the questions, look for the right opportunity to include some important thoughts that you have prepared in your research on the company. Do this carefully and do not upstage the interviewer.

Probing Questions

Probing questions may follow either the direct or indirect approach. These questions generally are unplanned and are used to clarify previous answers or to discover your attitudes and feelings on issues. An interviewer often uses probing questions to follow up on partial or superficial responses by directly indicating the kind of information he or she is seeking. Such probes might include, "That's interesting. I would like to know more about your thoughts on that" or "Why do you feel that way?" or "Give me a specific example of what you mean."

Expect a good interviewer to probe, especially on the second interview. Do not become defensive, but answer the questions by bridging them to the flow of your comments. At times an interviewer may ask a probing question while you are in the middle of a statement. If you answer it immediately, make a mental note to return to your original comments.

Stress-Related Questions

Stress questions, like those used in behavioral interviews, are designed to challenge you and make you think and respond quickly. They allow the interviewer to see if you can handle a tough environment. Some interviewers use the approach simply to change the pace of ordinary interviews.

True stress interviews are only appropriate when the job you are seeking poses regular stress and pressures. Otherwise, the approach is not useful. As Dr. Sandra Davis, a psychologist for the MDA Consulting Group, contends:

> Deliberate stress in interviews is only appropriate when the job requires one to deal day-to-day with interpersonal stress and challenge. If a job is stressful because of time pressures, then creating interpersonal pressure in an interview situation reveals nothing to me about the person's capacity to cope with pressure on the job. The information is useless, and I run the risk of alienating an otherwise outstanding candidate.[21]

The overall objective of an interviewer who uses stress questioning is to prevent you from using rehearsed answers. Your objective is to maintain your poise, respond in a calm and intelligent manner, and outlast the interviewer.

You may receive questions like, "We don't have an opening at the present time, but if we did, tell me why I should hire you" or "I have checked your grades and they are not that good. How can I know you can really perform?" These questions are obvious put-downs. Other questions might force you to leap from your mental position to a more creative mode. "See that chair you are sitting on? Sell it to me!" or "Evaluate this interview."

Interviewers who use stress questioning are more concerned with your method of handling the questions than with the answers themselves. Sometimes the interviewer uses nonverbal cues, rather than actual questions, to try to induce stress. An interviewer may look at you critically or establish no eye contact with you, looking out the window instead. He or she may sit in absolute silence while you walk in, waiting for you to start the discussion. Davis cites such an approach: "A common technique used by some is to ask a vague, open-ended question and then not respond in any way [to your answer], creating an awkward silence. You are left not knowing whether you answered the question, let alone whether you said something wrong."[22]

How can you prepare for possible stress questions? Do not concern yourself with what the interviewer wants to hear. Instead, mentally arrive at one or two answers and respond with those. Also, use pauses to your advantage. Five seconds may seem like an eternity, but it gives you valuable time to come up with an answer. When you see distracting nonverbal tactics, accept them for what they are and continue your discussion as if the interviewer was being polite. If you are greeted with silence, start with a line like, " I would like to tell you some things about my work experience." Your best device for handling a stress question is to be direct and respond with certainty.

Frequently Asked Questions

Be prepared for the most-frequently asked questions. According to job consultant Marcia Fox, 99 out of 100 college students put on their best dress-for-success outfits and polish their credentials, but they never make the effort to develop answers for such typical interview questions as:

- How did you happen to select your career choices?
- What are the qualities necessary for success in your field?
- What are your chief strengths?
- Why do you think you would like to work for our company?

As she states, "There's no way you can answer these questions without revealing whether or not you have done your homework about yourself, your career decisions, and the company."[23] Be ready for unexpected and seemingly irrelevant questions. In fact, anticipate at least one surprise question. You would be wise to spend considerable time developing answers to questions in the following four categories: ice-breaking, education-oriented, company-oriented, and you-oriented. Work on being spontaneous. Your answers should show your uniqueness and individuality.

Rehearse the questions in the preparation section. Some interviewing experts even advise carrying a list of questions about the company into the interview. At some point, you may want to ask the interviewer some of the questions. Asking good questions implies that you have done your homework. This will be discussed in more detail toward the end of the chapter.

Ice-Breaking Questions
1. Tell me about yourself.
2. How would you describe yourself?
3. How would a close friend describe you?
4. What did you do over the weekend?
5. What are your hobbies?
6. How do you like to spend your free time?

Education-Oriented Questions
1. Why did you seek an advanced degree?
2. Why did you choose your college or university?
3. What did you learn in the advanced program that you did not learn as an undergraduate?
4. What led you to choose your major area of study?
5. What classes in your major area did you enjoy the most? Least? Why?
6. Are your grades a good indication of your ability?
7. If you were to start over, what would you change about your educational experience?
8. Do you have thoughts about seeking an additional degree?
9. How has your advanced program prepared you for a business career?
10. Describe your most-rewarding college experience.
11. What did you learn from participation in extracurricular activities?

Company-Oriented Questions
1. Why did you decide to seek a position with this company?
2. What do you know about us?
3. Are you seeking employment in a company of a certain size? Why?
4. With what criteria are you evaluating the company for which you hope to work?
5. In what ways do you think you can make a contribution to our company?
6. If you were hiring someone with an advanced degree for this position, what qualities would you look for?
7. Why should I hire you?

You-Oriented Questions
1. Did you work during college?
2. What work skills did you develop?
3. Have you ever quit a job?
4. What are your long-range and short-range goals and objectives? When and why did you establish these goals? How are you achieving them?
5. What specific goals, other than those related to your occupation, have you established for yourself for the next ten years?
6. What do you see yourself doing five years from now?
7. What do you *really* want to do in life?
8. What are your long-range career objectives?
9. How do you plan to achieve your career goals?
10. What are the most-important rewards you expect in your business career?
11. What do you expect to be earning in five years?
12. Why did you choose the career for which you are preparing?
13. Which is more important to you, the money or the opportunity?
14. What do you consider to be your greatest strengths and weaknesses?
15. What motivates you to put forth your best effort?
16. What qualifications do you have that will allow you to be successful in business?
17. How do you determine or evaluate success?
18. What two accomplishments have given you the most satisfaction? Why?
19. Do you do any charity or community work?
20. What major problem have you encountered and how did you deal with it?
21. What have you learned from your mistakes?
22. Do you like people? Do you believe people like you?
23. Do you prefer working with people or alone?
24. Do you have a geographical preference? Why?
25. Will you relocate? Does relocation bother you?
26. Are you willing to travel?
27. Are you willing to spend at least six months as a trainee?
28. Why do you think you might like to live in the community in which our company is located?

29. Can you accept constructive criticism?
30. Can you laugh at yourself?
31. How do you work under pressure? Give me an example.

Illegal or Unfair Questions

Illegal or unfair questions are occasionally raised during interviews, so be prepared to respond to such questions. In most of these instances, the interviewer is probably just being careless, but discrimination can arise. Since state and local antidiscrimination laws vary, you should check with the appropriate labor and human rights agencies in your area to find out how local laws compare to the federal versions. Contrary to popular belief, there is no list of questions that employers are forbidden by federal law to ask. However, court cases have held that certain questions have violated specific federal laws in specific instances.

Questions about race, color, age, sex, religion, national origin, marital status, childbearing plans, past arrests, alcohol and drug abuse, and credit history become illegal if answers are used to discriminate. When it comes to enforcement, the parameters of discrimination are wide.

If you are asked illegal or unfair questions, first consider the context of the questions and the interviewer. If you feel the interviewer was not aware of how the question was asked and is not being discriminatory, simply pass it off. Should the flow of the conversation continue to offend you, tactfully tell the interviewer that the question is not appropriate to ask and has no bearing on the job description.

If you feel, however, that you are the subject of discrimination by a company, you have two options: you can overlook the discrimination issue and hope that once you are hired you will have no additional problems; or you can call local enforcement agencies to push for your rights. The agencies would need substantial proof of discrimination to initiate a case against the company.

Table 5.2 presents fair and unfair pre-employment questions. You can use this information to determine when an interviewer is asking questions that may be biasing his or her views toward you.

Potential-Employment Tests

More employers are beginning to request that interviewees submit to employment tests prior to their making those candidates a job offer. Such a request usually is made during an interview. As an interviewee you need to realize that an employer may make such a request. You should understand the reason the tests are being used, which tests are commonly used, and the risks you face when taking such tests. The following section describes three types of employment tests: lie-detector, drug, and psychological.

Lie-Detector Tests

For years lie-detector testing was used to screen job applicants and to check employee honesty. But in 1988 the passage of the Employee Polygraph Protection Act (EPPA) banned the use of lie detectors, except polygraphs, in most private-sector

Table 5.2 Antidiscrimination Questions That Can and Cannot Be Asked

Subject	Fair Preemployment Questions (What they can ask you)	Unfair Preemployment Questions (What they cannot ask you)
Name	Have you ever worked for this company under a different name? Is any additional information relative to change of name or nickname necessary to enable a check on your work record? If yes, explain.	Original name of an applicant whose name has been changed by court order or otherwise. Maiden name of a married woman. If you have ever worked under another name, state name and date.
Address or duration of residence	Applicant's place of residence. How long a resident of this state or city?	None.
Birthplace	Can you submit a birth certificate or proof of U.S. Citizenship if you are employed?	Birthplace of applicant. Birthplace of applicant's parents, spouse, or other close relatives.
Race or color	None.	Complexion or color of skin. Coloring.
Age	Are you between 18 and 65 years of age? If not, state your age.	How old are you? What is your date of birth?
Sex	None.	A preemployment inquiry as to sex on an application form is unlawful.
Marital status	Can you meet the specific work schedule, or do you have activities or responsibilities that may hinder meeting the requirements?	Are you married? Single? Divorced? Where does your spouse work? What are the ages of your children, if any?
Religion	Under special circumstances an applicant may be advised of normal hours and days of week required by the job to avoid possible conflict with religious or other personal convictions.	Inquiry into an applicant's religious denomination, religious affiliations, church, parish, pastor, or religious holidays observed. An applicant may not be told: "This is a Catholic, Protestant, or Jewish organization."
National origin	What languages do you read, speak, or write fluently? (only if pertinent to job)	Inquiry into applicant's lineage, ancestry, national origin, descent, parentage, or nationality. Nationality of applicant's parents or spouse. What is applicant's mother tongue?

(continued on next page)

Table 5.2 Antidiscrimination Questions That Can and Cannot Be Asked (continued)

Subject	Fair Preemployment Questions (What they can ask you)	Unfair Preemployment Questions (What they cannot ask you)
Citizenship	Are you a citizen of the United States? If not a citizen of the United States, do you intend to become a citizen of the United States? If you are not a U.S. citizen, have you the legal right to remain permanently in the United States? Requirement that applicants state whether they have ever been interred or arrested as an enemy alien.	Of what country are you a citizen? Whether an applicant is a naturalized or a native-born citizen. The date when the applicant acquired citizenship. Requirement that applicant produce naturalization papers or first papers. Whether applicant's parents or spouse are naturalized or native-born citizens of the United States. The date when such parents or spouse acquired citizenship.
Language	Inquiry into languages applicant speaks and writes fluently. What foreign languages do you read fluently? Write fluently? Speak fluently?	Inquiry into how applicant acquired ability to read, write, or speak a foreign language.
Education	Inquiry into the academic, vocational, or professional education of an applicant and the public and private schools he or she has attended.	None.
Experience	Inquiry into work experience. Inquiry into countries applicant has visited.	None.
Character	Have you ever been convicted of any crime? If so, when and where, and what was the disposition of offense?	Have you ever been arrested? (An employer's use of individual's arrest record to deny employment would, in the absence of business necessity, constitute a violation of the human rights law.)
Relatives	Names of applicant's relatives already employed by this company.	Names, addresses, ages, number, or other information concerning applicant's children or other relatives not employed by the company.
Disability	Can you perform specific job functions?	Do you have a disability? Have you ever been treated for any of the following diseases? (List diseases.) Has any member of your family ever had any of the following diseases? (List diseases.)

(continued on next page)

Table 5.2 Antidiscrimination Questions That Can and Cannot Be Asked (concluded)

Subject	Fair Preemployment Questions (What they can ask you)	Unfair Preemployment Questions (What they cannot ask you)
Notice in case of emergency	Name and address of person to be notified in case of an accident or emergency.	None.
Military experience	Have you ever been a member of the armed services of the United States or in a state militia? If so, did your military experience have any relationship to the position for which you applied?	None.
Organizations	Are you a member of any clubs, organizations, and so forth (exclude organizations for which the name or character indicates the race, creed, color, or national origin of its members).	List all clubs, societies, and lodges to which you belong.
References	Who suggested that you apply for a position here?	None.
Photograph	May be requested after hiring for identification purposes.	Requirement that an applicant affix a photograph to the employment form at any time before hiring, or at his or her option.
Arrest Record	Have you ever been convicted of a crime? (Applicant cannot be denied employment because of conviction, unless hiring would poise unreasonable risk or there is direct relationship between offense and job.)	Have you ever been arrested?

settings. Under limited circumstances, and with procedural safeguards, banks and other private-sector employers may still give polygraph tests to their employees. These must be limited to specific internal investigations and post-termination decisions to prosecute an employee for dishonest acts, however.[24]

Drug Tests

The American Management Association (AMA) runs a yearly survey on workplace testing. When the survey was first conducted in 1987 only 21 percent of the responding companies tested for drug usage. By 2001, 67 percent had drug tests in place and used it as a component of their policy. The increase was due to five factors:

1. Department of Transportation (DOT) and Department of Defense (DOD) regulations which, with local and state legislation, mandated testing in certain job categories;
2. The practical effects of the Drug Free Workplace Act of 1988;
3. Court decisions that recognize an employer's right to test both employees and job applicants in the private sector;
4. Action by insurance carriers to reduce accident liability and control health care costs; and
5. Corporate requirements that vendors and contractors certify that they have a drug-free workplace.[25]

Work categories determine the following frequency of corporate drug testing in 1999.

Manufacturers (89 percent) lead the service sector (67 percent). Within the service sector, 88 percent of transportation firms test; they are most affected by DOT regulations. Elsewhere, testing is performed by 71 percent of wholesalers and retailers, 55 percent of business service providers, 47 percent of financial service providers, and 69 percent of general service providers. In the public sector, 83 percent of respondent organizations test, compared with 77 percent of private sector firms.[26]

If you select work in the above areas you can expect random drug-test notification.

Personality and Psychological Tests

Employers increasingly realize that productivity, teamwork, and workplace harmony are the result of employees who easily fit into the organization's culture and climate. As a result the use of psychological tests has risen, albeit slowly. The 2001 AMA survey on psychological workplace testing found that 29 percent of employers require some form of psychological measurements. For job applicants, 11 percent use tests, and to evaluate current employees, 7 percent make use of such tests. The AMA survey listed five specific categories of measurement: cognitive ability, interest inventories, managerial assessments, personality measurements, and physical stimulation of job tasks.[27]

Certain industries are more prone than others to use such measurements. According to one source, ". . . more than 25 percent of companies filling IT positions assess candidates' personalities before making a job offer. Assessments range from multiple-choice questions for junior positions to an evaluation that could last up to four hours and include an interview with a behavioral psychologist for the most senior positions."[28]

The employee psychological test is a paper-and-pencil questionnaire designed to identify the right employee for the right job. The organizations who use such tests believe that the profile that results describes the candidate's values and beliefs, which in turn can objectively be compared to the company's profile of the ideal candidate for the position.

There are definite advantages of testing. A test can provide information on an individual's overall intellectual ability; basic skills, interests and inclinations; and personality characteristics. Tests can be very economical, especially if they result in hiring an employee who is committed, has improved performance, and is matched to the job. Some of the more-popular tests are Cattell 16 Personality Factor Questionnaire (16-PF); Gordon Personal Profile (GPP); Gordon Personal Inventory (GPI); Kostick Perception and Preference Inventory (PAPI); Myers-Briggs Type Indicator (MBTI); California Psychological Inventory (CPI); Personal Profile Analysis (PPA); PAL Personality Profile System (PPS); Performax Personal Profile System Personality; Poppleton-Allen Sales Aptitude Test; and several forms of the Occupational Personality Questionnaire. All of these tests are self-appraisal inventories that are reported to be useful in selection and training.[29]

To avoid being embarrassed if a future employer asks you to submit to one of these tests, there are two things you should do prior to the interview. First, know whether testing is the norm for new hires or promotions in the industry in which you are applying for employment. Second, understand the consequences of refusing to take a test. While refusing may guarantee your privacy, it may also cause you to not get the job.[30]

Practicing for the Interview

With your preparation complete, you are now ready to practice for your interview. Rehearsing is really the last stage in preparation. If you have been previously employed or if you have already gone through several interviews, you will be tempted to skip this part. Keep in mind, however, that every interview is a new performance and you must be ready for the task. True professionals in every walk of life, from music to sports to speaking, prepare and practice for the big event. When they experience anxiety they practice even harder to assure themselves that they are prepared, they keep a positive mental attitude, and they communicate positive nonverbal messages while remembering what they want to say to the interviewer.

Practice includes both mental and oral rehearsals. Mentally picture yourself walking into an interview, engaging the interviewer with a smile, firmly shaking hands, sitting in front of the interviewer, successfully answering each question, projecting a positive image, and smoothly leaving the room. Practice walking and talking with authority—not cockiness—and develop an air that vibrates with the sense that you feel good about yourself. Play and replay that positive mental tape many times prior to the interview. Act out each imagined behavior characteristic during the actual interview.

Making the Interview Count

When the big day arrives, you want the effort you have put into the preparation and practice segments of your interview to pay off. In this section, you will see how the location, your dress, your body image, and your communication will help you present the right image and sell the interviewer on the fact that you are the right candidate for the job.

The Interview Location

The majority of interviews occur either at a job placement center, on a college campus, or at a company office. You will be able to preview the placement center interview rooms prior to your campus interviews. If you are invited to the company location, you can discern important information about the company and its culture by observing the physical layout. Remember that the majority of information received in any message is nonverbal. Look, listen, and be aware of the features listed below; then let the information you learn guide you in the asking and answering of your interview questions.

The Grounds
Is the office in a downtown high-rise building, an industrial park, or a country-club setting? Each communicates a different message to you and to the employees.

The Aesthetics
Are the rooms airy and bright, or dull and dingy? Is the color scheme of the walls and carpet pleasing? Do windows offer pleasant views and sunlight? Are plants and artwork apparent? Do you feel comfortable there?

Noise Level
Do you detect a quiet hum or a loud clatter? Do phones ring constantly, or do office workers carry on loud conversations? Is this a place where you would like to work?

Floor Plan
How are the offices and departments arranged? Is there an open office system with partitions or permanent walls? Can you picture yourself in this type of environment?

The First Five Minutes: Forming a Positive Impression

The job interview has two critical segments. If you create the wrong impression in the first part, your chances of getting the job are slim, regardless of how well you perform in the second. Research indicates that most interviewers make up their minds about a job applicant in the first thirty seconds. Psychologists call this thirty-second decision the **halo effect.** It refers to the first impression an applicant makes upon an interviewer.[31] One study showed that if an interviewer had a negative impression about an applicant after the first five minutes, that person was not hired 90 percent of the time. If, however, the impression was positive, the applicant was hired 75 percent of the time.[32] The image you translate into the mind of the interviewer is how that person believes you will behave once you are hired. Work hard to make the image positive and accurate.

How can you create that positive impression? Frame the interview before it occurs. Mentally structure and prepare everything you will say and do during the event.

Arrive on time for the interview. Lateness creates a poor impression that is almost impossible to overcome. Be courteous, enthusiastic, confident, and prepared.

Remember the interviewer's name, and never address him or her by the first name. Practice and state the name several times and be sure to pronounce it correctly. Consider asking for a business card, to which you can refer if you have difficulty with the name. Have an extra copy of your resume, and literature about the company, especially if you wish to refer to them in a question. Have a pen and paper handy in case you want to make notes.

Handling Anxiety

Being prepared is the best prescription for overcoming anxiety. but if you suddenly become fearful, don't panic. Breath deeply and think of it as an adventure. You don't have to respond immediately to questions. Pause for a few seconds. Mentally outline the question, just as you rehearsed, and then communicate sincerely with the interviewer. Stay in a state of relaxed concentration. Quiet the negatives in your mind, draw on the specifics you have prepared, breathe slowly and deeply, and communicate like a pro. Remember, lots of entertainers, athletes, and businesspeople feel anxiety while performing and have to shift to a state of relaxed concentration. Usually the audience never knows about the anxiety unless the anxious person shares the fact. Keep the old adage in mind, "Never let them see you sweat."

Appropriate Dress

Dress appropriately for the interview and the profession. In the past most professional jobs required a suit, sport coat, and tie. Today, many industries have virtually abandoned the corporate uniform. A 1999 survey of 3,700 executives found 40 percent saying suits and ties may disappear entirely in a few years.[33] So what should you wear? Call the company receptionist or ask your interviewer what is apropos. "The purpose of the interview is to get to know you better. You and your accomplishments—not your clothes—should leave the lasting impression. When in doubt, your best bet is to stick with a suit or appropriate business attire."[34]

Here is what some interview advisors list for appropriate dress. These suggestions are not hard rules but only safe suggestions from numerous interviewers.

Men

- Appear clean-shaven or have facial hair neatly trimmed.
- A suit is the first choice for men. Choose a dark-colored suit in navy or gray. Brown is usually unacceptable and black is too formal. Pick pinstripes or solid colors.
- Wear a navy sport coat with beige or gray slacks, if suit is not available.
- The best shirt colors are white, light blue, tan, or yellow. A pointed collar is the traditional business style with button-down collars looking more casual. Make sure the shirt fits well and is neatly ironed.
- A tie is necessary and should be darker than your shirt.
- The favored shoe style is a conservative lace. The best color is black, brown, or burgundy and should match the belt. Make sure they are well shined and worn with dark socks.

Women

- A conservative, solid-colored or pinstripe suit is smart. The best colors are black, navy, gray, tan, or brown.
- A business dress with a jacket, or a tailored pantsuit is also acceptable.
- The recommended skirt length is knee length.
- A blouse with a neutral color like white or beige is advised. Avoid bright colors and loud prints.
- Jewelry should be conservative; only one ring per hand. Avoid anything that jingles. Only one earring per ear is also advised.
- Hair should be neatly combed and off the face.
- Wear light shades of lip coloring and nail polish.
- Avoid wearing heavy perfume or cologne.
- Shoes should not be open-toed or open-heel, with heels at two inches or less. Coordinate shoes with your ensemble.
- Wear hosiery that is close to skin color.

Body Language

Be aware of your body language. Walk erect and with purpose. Deliver a firm handshake, sit straight but at ease in your chair, smile warmly, and maintain eye contact with the interviewer. In fact, treat everyone you meet with courtesy. You never know when the interviewer might ask the receptionist for an impression of you as a person.

Don't chew gum in an interview. It is also best not to smoke, even if the interviewer gives you permission. If the interview is held in a reception format, drink very little alcohol. In fact, it is probably best to stick with a soft drink, juice, or club soda.

During the interview, don't become lethargic. Be alert and enthusiastic. Your energy button should be on from the moment you walk in the door. Strive to be constantly up and active as you listen to and talk with the interviewer. It's a good idea to avoid eating a heavy meal before an interview. If you have a tendency to get the jitters after drinking lots of coffee, limit your intake before the interview. Avoid indicating nervousness by wringing your hands, playing with your hair, or tapping your pen. Speak clearly. Constantly be aware of the image you are projecting.

Communication Pattern

During the interview display a courteous and active interest in the interviewer, the job, and the company—even if you sense a few minutes into the interview that your match-up with the company is wrong. Remain flexible and open-minded.

Help the interviewer during the discussion by avoiding a yes-and-no answer pattern. Listen. Avoid talking too much. Concentrate on the employer's words, tone of voice, and body language. As you are interviewing actively think about keeping your answers short. Each response should be between 30 seconds to one minute, unless you are asked to elaborate. Even then, constantly be aware of the length of your responses.

Table 5.3 Questions for the Interviewer

About the Organization
- What is it about this organization that attracted you and has kept you here?
- How would you describe your organization's style of management?
- How will industry trends affect this organization within the next three to five years?
- How does the organization define a successful individual?
- What is the method of feedback/evaluation used by this organization?
- What do you see as your organization's strengths and weaknesses?

About the Position
- Can you describe recent projects on which a person in my position has worked?
- What is the common career path for people entering the organization in this position?
- How are people trained or brought up to speed with regard to their responsibilities?
- What type of person tends to be successful in this position? What type of person are you looking for?
- How and when is performance evaluated?

Inappropriate Questions
- What salary can I expect?
- How much vacation time will I accrue?
- Are you willing to pay for graduate school?

Source: Adapted from: Job Search Strategies: Interview Preparation. (n.d.). Stanford Career Center, at http://www.stanford.edu/dept/CDC.

Work on making the interview a two-way dialogue. Be prepared to ask pertinent questions about the company or job that cannot be answered by looking in the company brochures. Table 5.3 presents a list of questions you can ask the interviewer. Examine the list and then add your own to each interview.

As you listen avoid the routine of note-taking, unless the interviewer wishes you to remember the name of a person, a book, dates, or other items. If you feel the need to write down information, do it quickly and with a professional look, or do it immediately after you finish the interview and exit the room. Always convey the impression of confidence and control.

Don't be conceited, arrogant, overbearing, or overly aggressive in your attitude and responses. While confidence is contagious and most interviewers are impressed by it, avoid arrogance and brashness which are immediate turnoffs. Avoid overusing "I." Many interviewees will say, "I did this, I did that, I accomplished." Overuse of "I" can cause an interviewer to be cautious. Try using the "we" and "you" approach instead.

Don't lie. Your nonverbal expressions give you away, but even if they do not, it is not worth the risk. Most companies fire a person immediately when a lie or misrepresentation is discovered.

Don't become defensive or hostile if the interviewer puts you under fire. Remain courteous, endure the stress, and finish the interview on as positive a note as possible. However, you should always preserve your dignity. If you feel the interviewer is belligerent and is placing you in a degrading position, get up and walk out.

Salary questions are best left until the second interview, or if you are immediately offered a job. Be sure that you are familiar with the salary ranges for the particular job for which you are interviewing.

Watch for verbal and nonverbal signals that the interview is over. Do not continue to talk, but rather work with the interviewer on controlling the time frame, especially if you are in a placement center. At the end of the interview, express your interest, or lack of, in the job. If you want the job be assertive and *ask for it*. If you do not like the company, but you are offered the job, turn it down—it can be a pleasant experience.

Don't Bad-Mouth Your Previous Employer

Answer all questions with a positive tone and in a professional manner. Never let yourself be drawn into a detailed discussion where you might say unfavorable things about your previous employers or other companies. Never bad-mouth your previous employer or complain about the working conditions you experienced. Always leave the impression that you are a positive thinker and a pleasant and professional person.

When you finish each interview congratulate yourself on the accomplishment that you made. Then as soon as possible review the entire event. What went right? What went wrong? What were you most proud of? Did the interviewer receive an accurate understanding of who you are and what you can do for the company? Which questions did you boggle? On which questions were you able to give brilliant answers?

Take what you have learned from the review, make necessary changes, relax, and prepare for the next challenge.

Notes

1. Monaco, D. (n.d.). Preparation for the interview. Monster Career Center. (p. 1). Retrieved September 6, 2002, at **http://contentmonster.com/jobinfo/interview/rehearse/**
2. Austin, V. A. (1999, Spring/Summer). The view from the other side of the desk. *Managing Your Career*, 19.
3. Eyler, D. R. (1999). *Job interviews that mean business: Turn interviews into jobs*, 35. New York: Random House.
4. Kennedy, J. L. (2002, March 17). Customize each interview pitch. *The Dallas Morning News*, 7-L.
5. Myron, D. (1999, May 24). Job interviewing—keeping employees all in the family. *Varbusiness*, 40.
6. Besson, T. (1999, July 31). Corporate culture—a candidate's checklist. *National Business Employment Weekly*, 15–16.
7. Austin, V. A. (1999, July 31). Clueless about interviewing. *National Business Employment Weekly*, 30.
8. Byrne, J. (1990, September 17). All the right moves for interviews. *Business Week*, 156.

9. Apynys, P. (1995, August 6). How to survive a nontraditional interview. *National Business Employment Weekly*, 15.
10. Eyler, D. R. (1992). *Job interviews that mean business*. (p. 91). New York: Random House.
11. Apynys, p. 15.
12. *Ibid*.
13. *Ibid*.
14. Case interviewing. (n.d.). Publication of University Career Services, Northwestern University. Retrieved April 2, 2002, at **http://www.stuaff.nwu.edu/usc/Students/job-skills/case.htm**
15. Interview practice: overview. (n.d.). Bain & Company. Retrieved September 30, 2002, at **http://205.134.84.25/bainweb/join/interview/practice_overview925.asp**
16. Case study tips. (n.d.). McKinsey & Company. (p. 3). Retrieved September 6, 2002, at **http://www.mckinsey.com/careers/apply/interviewingtips/casestudy/index.asp**
17. Ouellete, T. & Cole-Gomolski, B. (1998, April). Hiring managers turn to video. *Computer World*, 29.
18. Lublin, J. S. (1999, April 27). Hunting CEOs on a 32-inch screen. *The Wall Street Journal*, B1.
19. Bajaj, V. (1999, November 25). Face-to-face job interviews get clicking online. *The Dallas Morning News*, D1–2.
20. Davis, S. L. (1986, Spring). How to handle the stress interview. *Business Week's Guide to Careers*, 28.
21. *Ibid*.
22. Fox, M. (1985, Spring). Interview do's and don'ts. *Business Week's Guide To Careers*, 54.
23. Ruegger, D. (1991, November–December). When polygraph testing is allowed: Limited exceptions under the EPPA. *Banking Law Journal*, 555–564.
24. Greenberg, E. (Ed.). (2001). 2001 AMA survey on workplace testing: medical testing. A research report summary by the American Management Association. Retrieved September 28, 2002, at **http://www.amanet.org/research/summ.htm**
25. Greenberg, E. (Ed.). (1995). 1995 AMA survey: Workplace drug testing and drug abuse policies. A research report by the American Management Association.
26. Greenberg, E. (Ed.). (2001). 2001 AMA survey on workplace testing: Basic skills, job skills, psychological measurement. A research report summary by the American Management Association. Retrieved September 28, 2002, at **http://www.amanet.org/research/summ.htm**
27. Sierpina, D. (1999, April 19). Personality plays bigger role in IT recruitment. *Information Week*, 152.
28. Sahl, R. J. (1990, December). Probing how people think. *Personnel Journal*, 48–56.
29. *Ibid*.
30. Brothers, J. (1986, November 16). How to get the job you want. *Parade Magazine*, 4.
31. Bakeman, M., *et al.* (1991, November). *Job seeking skills reference manual*, 3rd ed., 57. Minneapolis, MN: Minnesota Rehabilitation Center.
32. Hayes, C. (1999, February). Casual for an interview. *Black Enterprise*, 73.
33. Leonard, B. (1999, January). Apparel in peril: Suits and ties are wearing thin. *HR Magazine*, 20.
34. Dress for success. (n.d.). Career Planning and Placement Brochure. Viterbo University. Retrieved September 14, 2002, at **http://www.viterbo.edu/academic/as/cpp/dress.html**

Index

Accenture, 81
Acceptance letters, 71, 72
Accomplishments, 24, 25
Acknowledgment letters, 71
Action verbs, 25, 26–27
America's Job Bank, 48
Analytical skills, 83
Antidiscrimination questions, 91–93
Anxiety, 97
ASCII resumes, 52, 55
Assessments. *See* Self-assessments and inventories
Assignment interviews, 80–81

Bain & Company, 81, 82, 84, 85
Behavioral interviews, 79–80
Besson, Taunee, 77
Body language, 98
Boeing, 15
Bolles, Richard, 16–17, 46–47, 49
Booze Allen & Hamilton, 81
Boston Consulting Group, 81, 85
Brain teasers, 81–82

Campbell Interest and Skills Survey, 13
Career Builder, 48
Career centers, 1–5, 16
Career Interests Game, 16
Career planning, 1–18
  college career center, 1–5
  occupational investigation, 16
  self-assessments and inventories, 5–16
Case interviews, 81–85
Chan, Savio, 77
Chronological-functional resumes, 31, 34
Chronological resumes, 28–29, 30, 37
Cisco Systems, 46
Co-op programs, 2

Cold-call letters, 68, 69
Communication skills, 83
Community activities, 25
Company homework, 76–78
Company-oriented questions, 89
Company values, 13, 14–15, 77–78
Consulting firms, 81
Correspondence. *See* Letters
Counseling, 2
Cover letters, 55, 64–67
Curriculum vitae (CV), 35, 39–40

Davis, Sandra, 87
Deloitte Consulting, 81
Diagnostic skills, 83
Dice.Com, 48
Direct questions, 86
Discrimination, 90, 91–93
Dress, 97–98
Drug tests, 93–94
Duties, 24

E-mail cover letters, 55
E-mail resumes, 52, 55–59
Education, 23–24, 88
Electronic resumes, 45, 49–60
  e-mail resumes, 52, 55–59
  online Web resumes, 59–60
  scannable resumes, 49–54
Elyer, David, 76
Employment section, 24–25
Ethics, 42–43, 77
Expanded data sheet, 40
Experience section, 24–25
Extra-curricular activities, 25
Extrinsic values, 9
Eyler, D.R., 80

First impression, 96–97
Flip Dog, 48
Follow-up interviews, 78–79
Fox, Marcia, 88
Frameworks, 83–84
Freshman year, 3–4

Functional cases, 82
Functional resumes, 28, 29, 31, 32–33, 38
Functional skills, 8

Gallup Organization, 15
Global resumes, 43
Goals, 3

Halo effect, 96
Heidrick & Struggles, 85
Holland's Self-Directed Search, 13, 16
Honors section, 28
Hot Jobs, 48
HTML resume, 59–60

Ice-breaking questions, 88
Illegal questions, 90, 91–93
Intel, 15
Interest inventories, 13, 16
International resumes, 43
Internships, 2
Interviews, 2, 70–71. *See also* Job interviews
Intrinsic values, 9
Inventories. *See* Self-assessments and inventories

Job databases, 48, 59
Job interviews, 75–101
  anxiety, 97
  assignment interviews, 80–81
  behavioral interviews, 79–80
  body language, 98
  case interviews, 81–85
  communication pattern, 98–100
  dress for, 97–98
  first impression, 96–97
  follow-up interviews, 78–79
  location of, 96
  potential-employment tests, 90, 93–95
  practicing for, 95
  preparing for, 75–78

103

Job interviews, *continued*
  previous employers, 100
  questioning approaches, 86–90, 99
  screening interviews, 78
  social interviews, 79
  videoconferencing interview, 85–86
Job offers, 71–73
Job questions, 17
Job-related skills, 6
Johnson & Johnson, 15
Jung, Carl, 6
Junior year, 4–5

Keirsey Temperament Sorter, 6
Key-word resumes, 51
Key words, 49–51

Letters, 63–74
  acceptance letters, 71, 72
  acknowledgment letters, 71
  cold-call letters, 68, 69
  cover letters, 55, 64–67
  declining an offer, 71–73
  format of, 63–64
  interview requests, 70–71
  self-descriptive words for, 66
  thank-you letters, 68–70
Lie-detector tests, 90, 93

Market sizing, 82
McKinsey & Company, 81, 82, 84–85
Microsoft, 15, 51
Military service, 28
Mission, 3, 77
Monster Board, 48
Montgomery, Stephen, 6
Motivators, 17
Myers Briggs Type Indicator, 6, 95

Nation Job Interview, 48
Net-Temps, 48

Objectives, 3, 17, 21–23
Occupational investigation, 16
Occupational skills, 6
OCR software, 49
Offers, 71–73
Online job searching, 45–49
Online Web resumes, 59–60
Open questions, 86
Organizational values, 13, 14–15, 77–78

PDF resumes, 60
Personal background, 28
Personality inventories, 5–6
Personality tests, 94–95
Placement center interviews, 70–71
Please Understand Me (Keirsey), 6
Polygraph, 90, 93
Potential-employment tests, 90, 93–95
  drug tests, 93–94
  lie-detector tests, 90, 93
  personality and psychological tests, 94–95
Previous employers, 100
Price Waterhouse Coopers, 81
Probing questions, 86–87
Psychological tests, 94–95

Questions, 17, 86–90, 99
Quintessential Careers, 16

Recruiting, 2, 46
References, 2, 28
Resumes, 19–44
  appearance of, 40, 42
  ASCII format, 52, 55
  chronological-functional resumes, 31, 34
  chronological resumes, 28–29, 30, 37
  constructing, 35, 40–43
  contents of, 19–28
  curriculum vitae, 35, 39–40
  e-mail resumes, 52, 55–59
  electronic resumes, 45, 49–60
  employer needs and, 20
  flaws in, 21
  functional resumes, 28, 29, 31, 32–33, 38
  global resumes, 43
  headings, 20
  HTML format, 59–60
  key-word resumes, 51
  length of, 40
  organizing content, 35, 40
  PDF format, 60
  sections of, 21–28
  skills emphasis resumes, 28, 34–35, 36
  truthfulness of, 44–45
  updating, 43
  Web resumes, 59–60
  wording of, 40, 41

Salary, 100
Scannable resumes, 49–54
Schein, Edgar H., 17
Screening interviews, 78
Self-assessments and inventories, 2, 5–16, 95
  interest inventories, 13, 16
  personality inventories, 5–6
  skill assessment, 6–9
  value assessment, 9–15
Senior year, 5
Skill assessment, 6–9
Skills, 6, 8, 83
  action verbs and, 26–27
  career objectives and, 22, 23
  in cover letter, 66
Skills emphasis resume, 28, 34–35, 36
Smith, Rebecca, 59, 60
Social interviews, 79
Sophomore year, 4
Southwest Airlines, 15
STAR method, 80
Strategy, 3–5
Strategy cases, 82
Stress questions, 87
Strong, E.K., Jr., 16
Strong Inventories, 6–7, 16
Summary statement, 23
Synovus Financial Corporation, 13

Testing, 2, 5–16, 90, 93–95
Thank-you letters, 68–70
Towers Perrin, 81
Transferable skills, 6

Unfair questions, 90, 91–93

Value assessment, 9–15
Values, 9, 13, 14–15, 77–78
Vault Consulting, 85
Videoconferencing interviews, 85–86
ViewCast.com, 86
Vision, 3
Volunteer activities, 25

Web resumes, 59–60
Web sites, 47, 48, 77
What Color Is Your Parachute? (Bolles), 16–17, 47
Work history, 24–25

Yes-no questions, 86
You-oriented questions, 89–90